Book of Bankruptcy

*The simple guide to bankruptcy
and other remedies to debt*

Robin Meynell

authorHOUSE®

AuthorHouse™
1663 Liberty Drive, Suite 200
Bloomington, IN 47403
www.authorhouse.com
Phone: 1-800-839-8640

© *2009 Robin Meynell. All rights reserved.*

No part of this book may be reproduced, stored in a retrieval system, or transmitted by any means without the written permission of the author.

First published by AuthorHouse 21 January 2009

ISBN: 978-1-4389-4629-0 (sc)

Printed in the United States of America
Bloomington, Indiana

This book is printed on acid-free paper.

The author has made every effort to ensure that the information given is accurate at the time of publication. The author and publishers cannot accept any liability for any errors, inaccuracies or changes in the law. Further, the author and publishers disclaim any liability arising from the use, or misuse of the information contained within this book.

Introduction

The 21st century has seen a social sea change in terms of attitudes to debt and bankruptcy. But as with all change some are better prepared to cope than others.

You may be applying for your first credit card or indeed already be bankrupt or considering bankruptcy, or one of the other options available to remedy debt; although the subject is daunting to many I hope you find my light hearted approach helps you better deal with debt and understand the impact that bankruptcy or the other options will have. In numerical terms, more people choose bankruptcy than the other available insolvency options and bankruptcy law creates criminal and civil offences for bankruptcy misconduct. My aim is ease of understanding of bankruptcy as the most common debt remedy and whilst this does not pretend to be an exhaustive guide it does cover the key issues that most people face. After reading BOB you should be better prepared to resolve any debt problems you encounter and get on with your life:

BOB delves into the fun-packed world of:

- Individual Voluntary Arrangements (IVAs)

- Debt Relief Order's (DROs)

- Debt Management Plans (DMPs)

- Bankruptcy – in particular;

    o   How the system works

    o   The consequences of misconduct

- o   That misconduct is the exception and not the rule

- o   What to expect when interviewed by one of the Insolvency Examiners, and what answers their questions look for

- o   A simple understanding of some of the complicated insolvency legislation

- o   Alternatives to bankruptcy or how to get your bankruptcy cancelled

- How to manage debt

Whilst I say fun, insolvency is far too dry a subject to make it so just by talking about what the law and the processes say. So, lets use a person to liven it up – meet Bob - he's in a bit of financial trouble and I thought you might find it illuminating to run through a series of different scenarios to show how the various decisions Bob is able to take, once he can see the mess he's in, can lead to very different outcomes – I hope that having read through these scenarios you will be better equipped to deal with debt.

You may be able to relate some of Bob's circumstances to yourself, family or friends. If so, I hope the scenario's help you clarify your understanding of your situation and allow you to shape the ultimate outcome to your best advantage.

Contents

Chapter 1
Individual Voluntary Arrangement (IVA).................... 1

Chapter 2
Debt Relief Order (DRO) 6

Chapter 3
Debt Management Plan (DMP) 9

Chapter 4
Bankruptcy – Who's who?............................ 11

Chapter 5
Bankruptcy – What's what?........................... 15

Chapter 6
Bankruptcy – How does it work? 36

Chapter 7
Bankruptcy – Sorting the sheep from the goats 60

Chapter 8
Bankruptcy – Demystifying the investigation............... 77

Chapter 9
Annulment (Cancellation) of bankruptcy 97

Chapter 10
How to manage debt 105

Epilogue 116

Appendix
Simple Individual Voluntary Arrangements (SIVA)
[Abolished Scheme]. 117

About the Author 121

Prologue

Bob & the Luxury Gap

Shortly after leaving school Bob was seduced by some sweet talking financial institutions. He could have all the luxuries he'd ever wanted and all he had to pay was a few percent every month – if it ever got too much to handle he could always take a loan, clear the lot and start again. Unfortunately, having done this a few times now, Bob's fallen behind on his payments to creditors.

Bob is struggling to make ends meet and his financial burden is adding considerable stress to both his and his family's lives. Bob knows if he buries his head in the sand, the situation will only get worse. To avoid any added pressure to pay his creditors, Bob has decided to look into the options available to clear his debts in full.

Bob had seen and heard advertisements on both TV and radio from companies claiming to have the answer to people's financial worries; however, looking for the easy answer is exactly what got Bob into his situation. Sensibly, Bob has decided to seek professional advice. So having made enquiries as to the available options, and following advice received from the Citizens Advice Bureau, Bob is now aware that there are four main options available to him:

- Individual Voluntary Arrangements (IVAs)
- Debt Relief Order's (DROs)
- Debt Management Plans (DMPs)
- Bankruptcy

Let's look at the options open to Bob, and the likely outcomes to each, more closely...

Chapter 1

Individual Voluntary Arrangement (IVA)

An IVA is a formal arrangement between an individual and his creditors. Whilst there is a public register of IVAs it has the advantage of avoiding the restrictions and obligations of bankruptcy, although as with bankruptcy there are legal consequences when entering into an IVA and it would be a criminal offence if Bob lied in his proposal. It is possible that creditors will not accept the terms set out in the IVA and if he doesn't comply with the terms of the arrangement itself he can be made bankrupt.

Bob sought advice from an Insolvency Practitioner (IP). It was all relatively easy, he visited The Insolvency Service's website at www.insolvency.gov.uk for a list of local IP's and when he telephoned his chosen IP he was told that the initial consultation was free of charge. Bob could alternatively have asked the Citizens Advice Bureau to provide him with names.

An IP is a person qualified to deal with the various insolvency procedures and many are also qualified accountants or solicitors. In the first instance the IP offered informal advice as to the options available to Bob and the option of an IVA was considered. Bizarrely, the IP would have a different name depending on the stage of the process – At this moment he had no

1

title and was giving advice – if Bob went ahead and put a proposal to his creditors the IP would be called a 'Nominee' – and if the creditors said yes he'd change hats and be called a 'Supervisor'.

In order to determine whether an IVA was the correct option for Bob to remedy his debts, they analysed his personal circumstances and considered the following:

1. Bob's current employment status

Bob's employment status had a direct impact on whether an IVA was the most appropriate option for Bob. Particular circumstances where an IVA may be a preferable option to the alternatives such as bankruptcy are:

- If Bob was working in a public office an IVA may be a preferable option to take rather than bankruptcy. If Bob was made bankrupt the law would not allow him to work in certain public offices, until the bankruptcy was concluded.

- If Bob held a professional qualification such as for a solicitor or an accountant it is possible Bob may have his practising certificate suspended if made bankrupt.

- If Bob was a director of a limited company, an IVA may be a better option for Bob as a bankrupt needs permission from the court to be a director or to be involved in the management of a company.

In this example, Bob is a company director.

2. Fees

The IP discussed the likely costs of an IVA with Bob. Up to this point the IP was just acting as an advisor to Bob and it was explained to Bob that if he decided to go ahead with an IVA, then a proposal would be presented to creditors. The IP would then act as Bob's 'Nominee'.

The role of the Nominee is to compile a report on Bob's financial circumstances, including details of all assets and liabilities, and write up a proposal that the IP thinks Bob and his creditors will agree to. There is no guarantee that the creditors will accept Bob's proposal or Nominee and the creditors may ask for a different IP or amendments to his proposal. If the creditors accept the proposal, the IP's role would then change and he would become the 'Supervisor' of the arrangement.

It is important to note the change in the IP's role. Whereas to begin with the IP acts largely in Bob's best interests in assessing his financial circumstances and assisting Bob in his decision as to whether an IVA is the best option for him, once the IP draws up the proposal there are legal consequences. If Bob lied in the proposal he could go to jail for up to seven years. Although the IP will assist Bob where necessary when the proposal is being drawn up, it is Bob's responsibility to ensure that it is honest and complete.

The IP's fees will be set out in the proposal both for his acting as 'Nominee' and as 'Supervisor'. The Nominee's fees are likely to be for a fixed sum agreed between Bob and the IP prior to the proposal being written. As you can only estimate the time the IP will spend supervising the IVA, it is likely that the Supervisor's fees will be stated as an estimate in the proposal. Fees of the IP acting as Supervisor are therefore unlikely to be fixed. These are more likely to be charged on an hourly basis. Total fees payable will depend largely on the time taken for the terms of the proposal to be completed and the IP's involvement in any future events that may arise during the course of the IVA.

3. The proposal

If Bob decides to go ahead with an IVA and the proposal is then approved, it will become a legally binding contract between Bob and his creditors. There will need to be a 75% vote from creditors in favour of the proposal in order for it to go ahead. The 75% vote is based on the value of creditors, not the number of creditors. For example one creditor may amount to, in value, more than 75% of the total value of creditors. Therefore in this instance the one creditor's vote would be sufficient to agree the proposal.

Although a 75% vote in favour of the IVA proposal is required, the vote will be based on the number of creditors that choose to vote in response to the proposal. If a creditor chooses not to reply, then that debt will not be included within the vote. The requirement is that 75% of the creditors that vote accept the agreement. If a 75% vote in favour of the proposal is obtained then the IVA can go ahead, and the creditors that chose not to vote but were in receipt of the proposal will also be legally bound by the agreement.

It is likely that creditors will insist on there being a clause in the proposal stating that if Bob failed to maintain his payments as set out and agreed in the proposal then the Supervisor will petition for Bob's bankruptcy. It is therefore essential when considering the proposal that it is realistic, as if Bob is unable to meet his side of the agreement in the proposal it will almost certainly result in his personal bankruptcy.

If accepted, the proposal will be agreed for either full or part payment of creditors. If the agreement is to be made in part payment then it is likely that the agreement will be for $\underline{x}$ pence in the pound to be paid to creditors. For example, Bob may propose to pay 50p in the pound. Therefore, only £500 would be payable into the arrangement for every creditor to whom he owes £1,000. The IP's fees are usually taken out of the money paid in. So even though this results in a creditor owed £1,000 getting less than £500, Bob would still have honoured his side of the arrangement and the creditors could not come back for more.

Having considered all of the above Bob decided to go ahead with the option of an Individual Voluntary Agreement (IVA) with his creditors.

Bob discussed his financial position with the IP. He had to inform the IP of all income and his essential expenditure. Bob disclosed all assets to the IP.

Unlike bankruptcy where all assets (where not exempt) must be realised for the benefit of creditors, there is some leeway for Bob going for the option of an IVA. An IVA agreement can be flexible although creditors will expect to receive at least as much through an IVA as they would from bankruptcy. So when Bob disclosed a painting that he owns to the IP which was worth £1,000 but which held sentimental value, it was possible to word the agreement whereby creditors accepted that he was allowed to keep it.

In many cases IVA proposals are arranged so that monthly payments are made from a surplus income for a period of five years. As just mentioned, IVAs are flexible and it may be possible for the agreement to be arranged differently, such as payments from a third party.

Following a proposal having been written to the satisfaction of the IP, a meeting was arranged with Bob's creditors.

In IVA cases, an interim order is sometimes sought from the court. The purpose of the interim order is that it will prevent creditors from taking further action against the debtor (Bob) prior to the meeting of creditors. It is no longer a legal requirement to have an interim order in place prior to the meeting and these day's interim orders are only obtained if further action from a creditor is imminent. Bob did not seek an interim order.

Although Bob in theory does not have to attend the meeting of creditors, he was advised by the IP that he should as creditors may insist on changes to the proposal and if Bob were absent, it would not be possible to come to an agreement. Bob agreed to attend the meeting and a 75% vote of creditors was received in favour of the proposal.

Part of the agreement was that Bob would pay a fixed fee towards the IVA each month. Due to Bob owning a house and there being equity in the house (i.e. less the mortgage there is still value in the house), the final payment to be made would be the release of the equity in Bob's house. At the end of the arrangement, in order to make this final payment, Bob re-mortgaged his house to cover the equity. Obviously at this time Bob's monthly mortgage payments increased. However, his monthly payments towards the IVA had now ceased and Bob was now clear of all his unsecured debts (i.e. all creditors other than the mortgage debt secured against his property).

Chapter 2

Debt Relief Order (DRO)
[Expected date of implementation: April 2009]

A DRO, once available, will be the simplest, cheapest and very probably least stressful procedure. However, as you will see it will only be available under fairly restricted circumstances. A DRO will provide relief from debts obtained up to the date of the order. Similarly to bankruptcy the debtor will be discharged from his debts after twelve months from the date of the order.

The DRO is a government proposed alternative to the current options available to remedy debt, such as an IVA or bankruptcy. As this system (at the date of publication) is not currently available, all amounts and other information regarding the DRO are based on proposals only and may be subject to change.

There will be a cap of £15,000 set for the maximum level of debt that a person may have when applying for a DRO. This is based on unsecured debts. Creditors that hold security over assets such as a mortgagee over a property will retain the protection of their debt over the property.

It is proposed that anyone applying for a DRO will have less than £300 of assets. However, some assets similarly to bankruptcy may be excluded, examples being domestic items (e.g. Sofa, bed, etc) and tools of trade.

In this example, Bob is currently working as a Check-Out Assistant at the local supermarket and is receiving a minimal income. Bob decided to opt for the DRO as his creditors only total £12,000. Also Bob has no assets that could be sold for the benefit of his creditors.

Obtaining a DRO is likely to incur Bob a small cost, but this cost will be smaller than the fee that must be paid to be made bankrupt. The fee when petitioning for bankruptcy is currently set at £495 and it is believed that the cost to Bob to apply for a DRO will be no more than £100; this sum will be non-refundable.

The cost of a DRO is less than that of a bankruptcy order due to the fact that a large proportion of administrative work involved in bankruptcy cases will not be necessary in DROs. For example, there will be no assets for the Official Receiver to either protect or sell. It is unlikely that it will be decided Bob needs to be interviewed as his debts are so small. Due to the low level of debts it may also not be considered necessary to investigate the financial affairs of Bob to the same degree that they would be in a bankruptcy case.

If Bob were dishonest in his application for a DRO, then the order would be revoked and creditors could pursue their debt. If Bob's dishonesty were considered by the Official Receiver to be deliberate then Bob may be liable to prosecution or perhaps a restriction order similar to that in bankruptcy (explained in chapter 7).

To qualify for a DRO it is also required that Bob's surplus monthly income amounts to less than £50 per month. If Bob's surplus monthly income amounts to more than £50 then he may be in a position to make monthly contributions from his income to creditors. Such a method is used in bankruptcy and is known as an income payments agreement or order. Due to the DRO being set up for the simpler debtor cases, the smaller administrative costs involved do not support such a system.

In bankruptcy, the surplus income is based on Bob's monthly income less his essential monthly expenditure. An explanation of how to calculate the surplus income in bankruptcy can be seen in chapter 6. The calculation of surplus income for a DRO is likely to be similar but Bob would need to discuss this with his intermediary (see below).

Bob's monthly surplus income is under £50 and he qualifies for the option of a DRO.

The Official Receiver will be responsible for administering the DRO. When Bob applies for the DRO he has to apply via an intermediary such as the Citizens Advice Bureau (CAB) or Consumer Credit Counselling Service (CCCS). Bob does not attend the court as he would if petitioning for his own bankruptcy. The Intermediary discussed Bob's financial circumstances with him and looked at whether a DRO was the best option to take considering Bob's circumstances. Bob provided the intermediary with as accurate information as possible, clearly stating reasons for his insolvency and answering all questions in full. The Intermediary was then able to submit a web-based form to the Official Receiver applying for Bob's DRO.

The Intermediary's role will be only to offer advice and to assist in putting forward the application for a DRO. The sole responsibility as to whether a DRO should be made would lie with the Official Receiver.

Finally, as a measure of preventing people from taking advantage of the system by regularly getting their debts written off, it has been proposed that a DRO can only be obtained once every six years.

Chapter 3

Debt Management Plan (DMP)

A Debt Management Plan (DMP) is an informal arrangement between an individual and his creditors. The DMP is usually considered by those with few debts who hope to escape the need of entering into formal insolvency procedures such as in an IVA, DRO or bankruptcy.

Debt Management plans are often offered by debt management companies, such as those seen and heard advertised on the television and radio.

Following enquiries Bob had made with a debt management company, Bob found that an advantage of entering into a DMP over one of the formal arrangements with creditors is that once entered into he would not be listed on a public register. Therefore no one outside the arrangement need know of the agreement Bob had entered into with his creditors.

Bob discussed his financial circumstances with a counsellor from the debt management company and set up an informal proposal to make monthly payments into the plan. The counsellor explained that they would arrange the distribution of funds to creditors. It was also explained that the counsellor's fees for the arrangement would also be paid out of these monthly contributions. Bob was happy with the proposed arrangement as if creditors were to agree, then he would only be making one monthly payment which would amount to less than the current total monthly repayments he was incurring between his credit cards and loans.

Before deciding whether a DMP is the right option for Bob, the counsellor explained the potential pitfalls of a DMP:

- As a DMP is an informal arrangement with creditors, they are not legally bound by the agreement and can therefore choose to opt out of the arrangement at any time.

- Whilst a DMP may provide affordable monthly repayments for Bob to his creditors, over the course of the arrangement it is likely that Bob will be paying more over a longer period of time.

- It is likely that Bob will continue to be charged interest on his debts throughout the arrangement, though the debt management company may be able to agree with some of the creditors to freeze his interest.

- As Bob will be making smaller monthly contributions to each creditor, it is possible creditors may record this on his credit file.

Debt Management Schemes

When Chapter 4 of The Tribunal Courts and Enforcement Act 2007 comes into effect Bob will be able to enter into a formal debt repayment plan, which will stop creditors in the plan taking further action against him. He will be released from those debts once he has honoured all his obligations under the plan. Such an arrangement (at date of publication) is not currently available.

Chapter 4

Bankruptcy – Who's who?

Before we start running through the processes of bankruptcy, it is useful to have a brief understanding of the different people involved, and to understand what their role is in the bankruptcy process. Further more detailed explanations will be given throughout this book.

Who deals with the bankruptcy?

Trustee

Either the Official Receiver or an Insolvency Practitioner will be appointed as Trustee and will be responsible for the sale of assets and the distribution of funds to creditors.

Official Receiver (OR)

The Official Receiver is responsible for investigating the financial affairs of the bankrupt. He is also responsible for administering the bankruptcy and protecting the bankrupt's assets. If appointed as Trustee, the Official Receiver will also be responsible for the sale of assets and then ultimately distributing monies held in the bankruptcy estate to creditors.

The bankruptcy estate holds the total funds received in an individual bankruptcy case. These funds may be from cash held in the bankrupt's bank account and proceeds received from the sale of assets owned by the bankrupt.

Insolvency Practitioner (IP)

In most cases the Official Receiver is the appointed Trustee in a bankruptcy case. However, in some cases an Insolvency Practitioner will be appointed. In these instances the Insolvency Practitioner will be responsible for the bankrupt's financial affairs and it will be the IP's duty to sell assets and distribute funds to creditors.

Assistant Official Receiver (AOR)

The Assistant Official Receiver is exactly as his title states. He assists the Official Receiver in his duties. The Assistant Official Receiver also oversees the work carried out by the Examiners and Case Officers.

Examiners

Examiners will take the main role concerning a bankrupt's affairs. The Examiner will be the bankrupt's main point of contact and will be the person who will carry out any investigative work concerning the bankruptcy. There are three levels of Examiner with the Level 3 Examiners being the most senior.

The main roles of an Examiner are:

- to set a date and time to interview the bankrupt

- interview the bankrupt

- prepare a report to be sent to creditors

- inform all necessary parties of the bankruptcy order

- carry out all further investigation required

- if misconduct is found and proved after a full investigation, the Examiner will prepare a report to be reviewed by the Official Receiver. The report will then be sent to the Secretary of State (investigations carried out by the Examiner are explained later in this book). Although the report will be prepared and written by the Examiner, the report will be prepared in the name of the Official Receiver and the Official Receiver will remain responsible for its content.

- The Examiner will delegate work to the Case Officer

Level 1 Examiner

A Level 1 Examiner carries out the initial investigation into the affairs of bankrupts who have applied for their own bankruptcies (known as a debtor's petition) and they will deal with the day to day matters on assets and liabilities. Level 1 Examiners investigate the affairs of bankrupts who have not been trading a business and where there are no obvious matters that require a fuller analysis. However, if there are potential areas of misconduct they will pass the investigation to specialised Level 2 and Level 3 Examiners to look into the matter in more detail.

Level 2/Level 3 Examiner

A Level 2/Level 3 Examiner is a higher grade Examiner who investigates the affairs of bankrupts who have been made bankrupt after the petition of a creditor (known as a creditor's petition). The difference between the two grades is the complexity of the cases they administer. Level 2/Level 3 Examiners also investigate the affairs of bankrupts who have petitioned for their own bankruptcies and have traded a business or consumers who have been reckless or dishonest. Level 3 Examiners deal with the potentially more complex cases, usually where a bankrupt has been trading a business and therefore further work is required to establish the cause of the bankrupt's insolvency.

Robin Meynell

Case Officer

The Case Officer will carry out work assigned by Examiners. Such work would include following up receipts to letters sent from the Examiner.

Chapter 5

Bankruptcy – What's what?

At the risk of oversimplifying matters, Bankruptcy will mean that Bob's responsibility for his debts up to the date of the bankruptcy order will effectively be brought to an end. The creditors will instead "prove" in the bankruptcy and receive a dividend from assets (if any). Some debts are not "provable" in bankruptcy e.g. If Bob had any fines or a student loan these will likely remain with Bob despite the bankruptcy order having been made. All other debts will fall within the bankruptcy. Any debt that arose after the bankruptcy order was made is not a bankruptcy debt. Bankruptcy however cannot be explained in one paragraph and Chapters 5 to 9 give you an insight into the intricacies of bankruptcy and will prepare insolvents for the various different circumstances that lie ahead.

The following is a summary of the bankruptcy process from start to finish:

1. Bankruptcy Order made at court

2. Official Receiver's Office notified of order

3. Bankruptcy case allocated to Examiner and Case Officer

4. Documents sent to bankrupt for completion

5. Initial enquiries take place

6. Bankrupt interviewed (if considered necessary)

7. Trustee appointed

8. Report written and sent to creditors

9. Internal conduct report prepared by Examiner detailing his recommendation.

10. Possible further investigation and repercussions of any misconduct found

The above events are explained further through the eyes of Bob as follows:

1. Bankruptcy order made at court

There are two principal ways to become bankrupt.

Method 1

Bob can apply for his own bankruptcy. This is known as a 'Debtor's Petition' for bankruptcy.

In order to petition for his bankruptcy, Bob first calls his local court and requests a bankruptcy pack. A bankruptcy pack includes:

- Debtors bankruptcy petition

- Statement of affairs

- Guidance notes for completion of the statement of affairs

On receipt of this pack Bob completes the statement of affairs form in full. The statement of affairs is a comprehensive form that lists various questions regarding his financial affairs. The guidance form provided by the court provides basic guidance to the questions asked but does not provide an in-depth analysis of these questions and the possible repercussions your answers may cause. Accordingly, in Chapter 8 I provide explanations to the questions asked and offer guidance on answers to these questions.

Bob can either complete the Statement of Affairs form by hand (completing the form sent in the bankruptcy pack), or online. Bob decides to complete his statement of affairs online and visits the Insolvency Service Website at www.insolvency.gov.uk. The online form is known as i-solv. After completing the online form Bob prints out and signs the form.

Following completion of the statement of affairs form, Bob contacted his local court to book a hearing to be heard before the district judge. He also had to fill out a petition form formally saying he was insolvent and asking to be made bankrupt and go on oath to say that his statement of affairs was true and fair. At the hearing the district judge reviewed Bob's financial circumstances laid out in the statement of affairs form, and made a formal order making him bankrupt. The hearing was over quickly and did not last any longer than 10 minutes. Bob now waits to hear from The Insolvency Service who will be in contact with him in due course.

Bob paid £495 to the court in cash in order to be made bankrupt. This goes to pay a court administration fee of £150 and £345 deposit towards the Official Receiver's fee (the Official Receiver administers the bankruptcy following the making of the bankruptcy order). Bob feels it is slightly ironic that he should be expected to stump up such a fee when he is clearly not in a position to pay his other debts. However, this is necessary in order to be made bankrupt and Bob paid the fee to the court.

It is worth noting that some are exempt from the £150 court fee if they are claiming benefits and their gross annual income is less than £15,050. If you think you may be able to claim exemption from the court fee, ask the court to provide you with a copy of the court leaflet EX160A, 'Court fees – do you have to pay them?' Alternatively call your local court to discuss this. The rules for exemption and remission do not apply to the Official Receiver's deposit of £345; however, some charities provide assistance with paying the deposit and the Court or local CAB may be able to give details of charities in your area.

Method 2

A creditor (a person to whom Bob owes money) can apply for Bob's bankruptcy. This is known as a 'Creditor's Petition' for bankruptcy. By law, it is necessary for a creditor to follow the correct procedure when petitioning for bankruptcy. It is worth noting that anybody who is owed more than £750 can petition for a bankruptcy against any individual. Bob owed Sid's Kitchen Appliances Ltd £2,000.

Sid's Kitchen Appliances Ltd is one of Bob's creditors and has petitioned for Bob's bankruptcy. In order to make Bob bankrupt, they had to pay to the court £605 comprising a court administration fee of £190 and £415 deposit towards the Official Receiver's fee. As Bob had not applied to the court for the bankruptcy, Bob did not pay the fee.

2. Official Receiver's Office notified of order

Once the bankruptcy order has been made, the court will notify the Official Receiver's office of the bankruptcy order. On receipt of notification of the bankruptcy order, the Official Receiver allocates Bob's bankruptcy case to an Examiner and a Case Officer.

3. Bankruptcy case allocated to Examiner and Case Officer

At the Official Receiver's Office, each bankruptcy is categorised on the basis of its complexity and allocated to an Examiner with the appropriate level of knowledge and experience. The categorisation is for internal purposes only and Bob will not be notified of what case type his bankruptcy is to be considered as. Whilst the case type chosen is significant as to how

Bob's bankruptcy will be progressed, the categorisation will be reviewed and changed if circumstances change.

What do the different case types mean?

Put simply, investigation time costs money and there is no purpose to doing a detailed investigation of a simple case where the cause of failure is already clear.

A routine case is considered straightforward and little work is required from the Official Receiver's Office. This is likely in cases with minimal debts and no assets. A complex case may require more in depth analysis from the Examiner. An intermediate case falls somewhere in between.

The bankruptcy order made against Bob in *method 2* by Sid's Kitchen Appliances Ltd will be allocated as a 'complex' case. This is because all bankruptcy cases made through creditor's petitions are allocated as complex by default. The reason for this is that generally (but not always) bankruptcy orders made through creditors petitions are more involved, as the bankrupt is likely to have traded a business at some stage, therefore more time will be needed to be spent by the Examiner investigating the bankrupt's financial affairs.

Creditor's petitions tend to be made in relation to a trade debt. However, this is not always the case. It is again worth noting that anybody who is owed more than £750 can petition for a bankruptcy against any individual.

Where Bob applied for his own bankruptcy in *Method 1*, it is more likely that his case will be assigned as routine or intermediate.

In the case where Bob petitioned for his own bankruptcy it does not mean that his bankruptcy case will definitely be allocated as 'routine' or 'intermediate'. It may be allocated as a 'complex' case. One circumstance that may give rise to such an allocation would be in reviewing Bob's 'Statement of Affairs', the Assistant Official Receiver/Examiner has decided that there is something in the Statement of affairs that may require a more in depth review. Such things could be:

- If Bob has traded a business, either as a sole trader or in partnership with another at some stage in the last two years

- If Bob has been a director of a limited company in the last two years

- If Bob has admitted to gambling within the last two years

- If Bob has an exceptionally large level of assets or creditors

How would the case type affect Bob?

Routine case

If Bob's bankruptcy case is allocated as 'routine', he will not be required to be interviewed. The fact that Bob's case has been allocated as 'routine' means that 'The Official Receiver' is satisfied that no further information is required. This case will also presently result in an early discharge (explained later in this chapter). This case will be dealt with by a Level 1 Examiner.

Intermediate case

If Bob's bankruptcy case is allocated as 'intermediate', it has been decided that further information is needed and he will be required to be interviewed (usually by telephone) by a Level 1 or Level 2 grade Examiner. This interview will not go into great depth and the Examiner will only ask what are considered to be the essential questions to protect the assets, identify the creditors, determine the cause of failure and identify whether Bob can afford payments from income and if so how much. – Explained in Chapter 6.

The Examiner is essentially required to find out the above information and may well not ask Bob any further questions. The interview should not last more than 30 minutes, but if Bob has questions of his own it may take longer.

Complex case

If Bob's bankruptcy case is allocated as 'complex', the Examiner requires further information and Bob will be required to attend the Official Receiver's office for a face to face interview with a Level 2 or Level 3 grade Examiner. This will require an in depth interview and the Examiner will run through the completed statement of affairs (if as in *Method 1*, Bob applies for his own bankruptcy) or the completed Preliminary Information Questionnaire (if as in *Method 2*, a creditor petitioned for Bob's bankruptcy).

The interview is likely to last any time between 30 minutes and 2 hours.

4. Documents sent to bankrupt for completion

Once the case type has been decided, the Examiner will send to Bob the following documents:

- Appointment letter - if case allocated as 'intermediate' or 'complex'

- Questionnaire - If made bankrupt through the petition of a creditor. It is unlikely Bob will be sent a questionnaire if he petitioned for his own bankruptcy.

- Restrictions and obligations form

- Tax form

- Ethnic Monitoring form

- Comment card

These documents (other than the appointment letter and comments card) require completion and will need to be returned prior to the date of Bob's interview, as they will be the main focus of the interview.

These documents are explained below:

Appointment letter

A covering letter will be sent to Bob explaining the documents enclosed and requesting they be completed and returned. This letter will also state that either no interview is considered necessary at this time, or it will state a date and time that Bob must either be available for a telephone interview or to attend the Official Receiver's Office for interview.

Telephone interviews must be made on a landline telephone number. The Examiner will not interview Bob on a mobile telephone number. If a telephone interview is set, the Examiner will call Bob at the set time, not the other way around.

If Bob has been set a face to face interview, then Bob will be expected to attend the Official Receiver's office on the date and time set.

Three strikes and you're out

Bob is obliged under a court order to attend on the Official Receiver and cooperate. The Official Receiver is an officer of the court and will ensure Bob respects the court's order. If Bob is invited to attend the Official Receiver's office for a face to face interview he will usually be given a maximum of three opportunities to attend his appointment. If Bob fails to attend after three missed appointments then the Official Receiver will arrange for Bob's public examination. This will be a court hearing held at the local court in which Bob's bankruptcy order was made and Bob will be required to attend this hearing. If Bob does not attend, then it is likely Bob's discharge from bankruptcy will be suspended indefinitely until he chooses to comply. There may also be circumstances where the Official Receiver would seek a warrant for Bob's arrest.

If Bob's bankruptcy discharge is suspended then the restrictions and obligations (listed below) imposed on him as an undischarged bankrupt will remain with him until he cooperates with the Official Receiver sufficient to a warrant lifting the order; even then, if for example his discharge was suspended at three months into the order, following the lifting of the suspension, as bankruptcy ordinarily lasts for 12 months he will still have the remaining 9 months of his bankruptcy year to run.

If, when Bob is sent an appointment letter he calls the Official Receiver's office with a reasonable explanation as to why he cannot attend on this date, a further appointment letter will be sent with a new date for interview. This will delay the 'three strikes and you're out' process. However, Bob should attend and burying his head in the sand is no solution to his problems and could very well make things worse.

Questionnaire

If made bankrupt through a creditor's petition, Bob will be required to complete a questionnaire. This questionnaire is explained fully in chapter 8, and explains the purpose of some of the key questions asked and the consequences to a series of alternative answers given to these questions.

It is possible that if Bob was made bankrupt through his own petition that he will be asked to complete a questionnaire, however this is unlikely. In these instances, he will only be asked to complete a questionnaire if he was involved in the trading of a business. He would then be required to complete a different questionnaire (not so complex) that focuses on the business and employee details. This does not repeat the questions asked in his 'Statement of Affairs' which he will have already completed on the petition of his own bankruptcy.

Restrictions and obligations form

This form sets out the restrictions and obligations that Bob must adhere to whilst he is an undischarged bankrupt. The key points are summarised at the beginning of this form as follows:

- ➢ You must tell your Trustee within 21 days about any property that becomes yours and any increases in your income during your bankruptcy.

- ➢ You must not obtain credit of £500 or more, either alone or with another person from anyone without first informing that person that you are bankrupt. You may open a new bank or building society account but you should tell the bank or building society when opening the account (and must tell the bank or building society before incurring an overdraft) that you are bankrupt.

- ➢ You must not carry on business (directly or indirectly) in a different name from that in which you were made bankrupt without telling all those with whom you do business the name in which you were made bankrupt.

- ➢ You must not be concerned (directly or indirectly) in promoting, forming or managing a company, or act as a company director (whether or not you are formally appointed as a director), without the court's permission.

- ➢ You may not hold certain public offices.

- ➢ You may not hold office as a Trustee of a charity or a pension fund.

The form provides the law in greater detail on the above and other points. However, as long as Bob fully understands the summarised points listed at the front of the document, this covers most of the issues that affect him and that he really needs to know well.

Bob will be sent two copies of the restrictions and obligations form; one is to be kept for his own reference and the other is to be signed by Bob and countersigned by a witness and then returned to the Official Receiver's Office. When the Official Receiver receives the signed form he will keep a copy of the signed form on his file and will send the original signed copy to the court to be kept on their file as the court keep their own file of Bob's bankruptcy case.

Tax form

Bob will be required to sign a tax form; Signing this form means that he is effectively agreeing to his allowing the Official Receiver to request details regarding his personal tax history; Signing this form also means that he agrees that if any tax rebates are owing to him, that these monies will be paid into the bankruptcy estate (the pot of money to be distributed amongst creditors). Finally, once Bob has signed this form, this will act as a reminder to HM Revenue and Customs as to how to deal with his personal tax. The "No Tax" coding is explained in chapter 6.

Ethnic Monitoring form

Bob will be required to tick the relevant boxes on the ethnic monitoring form. This is for statistical purposes and helps the government monitor how their policies work in practice e.g. if every Jedi Knight received a BRO the government would need to check why the law prejudiced Jedi Knights.

Comment card

Bob will be sent a comment card. After the interview Bob may wish to complete this card to state how satisfied he was with the processes of bankruptcy. Despite the fact that he had been asked to explain his debts and insolvency Bob was quite surprised at how supportive and non judgemental the Examiner had been; He warmed to his Examiner and said he was very satisfied with the process on the comment card. Bob put his full name on the comment card to ensure that the comments did not remain anonymous.

5. Initial enquiries take place

Before any interview takes place, Bob may be contacted and required to answer some initial enquiries over the telephone. The main purpose of this is for the Examiner to identify any matters which require immediate attention e.g.:

- to ensure that Bob is not currently trading a business, as the Official Receiver does not have the power to trade a business

- to establish what assets are owned by Bob and if they need to be realised (sold) urgently.

If Bob was trading a business when the bankruptcy order was made, the Official Receiver has the power to close the business and dismiss all of Bob's staff. The Official Receiver or the Assistant to the Official Receiver will do this. If there is value in the business and the goodwill will be lost by closing the business, it may be that the best option is to allow the business to continue trading. As the Official Receiver does not have the legal authority (his powers are specifically listed in the Law and he can't exceed these) to run a business Bob will need to either temporarily close whilst he gets rid of the order (annuls it) or get someone appointed who can trade a business. In such instances the Official Receiver would look to appoint an Insolvency Practitioner to be appointed as Trustee in his place. The Insolvency Practitioner as Trustee will then be responsible for dealing with all asset-related affairs of Bob and his business.

As the Official Receiver cannot carry on a business, if Bob is self employed and has no assets but does employ a member of staff, then the Official Receiver will have to dismiss that member of staff. However, after the member of staff has been dismissed, Bob may start trading again and re-employ that individual. At first, this may seem daft, but you have to deal with the formalities of stopping and starting trade.

The initial enquiries will be carried out in the early stages of Bob's bankruptcy in order to find out what assets Bob owns. The need to find this information out early is because some assets may need to be realised as a matter of urgency. Such assets could be cash in the bank or perishable stock such as frozen food. Other assets such as the value in a property may need to be realised but not with such urgency, as the asset is unlikely to be going anywhere between now and the date Bob is to be interviewed.

Initial enquiry questions:

Bob will not be expected to know exact sums and to be able to answer questions with absolute certainty at this stage. The initial enquiries are likely to be carried out by telephone. If it is believed that Bob is trading a business and the Examiner is unable to contact Bob by telephone then Bob will be visited by the Examiner and the Official Receiver or Assistant Official Receiver.

During the initial enquiry stage, Bob will be asked questions on the following (if Bob has not been involved in any area the Examiner will note that and quickly move on):

- **Bankruptcy details**
    o Estimate your total liabilities (the total amount you owe to creditors)
    o Estimate how many creditors you have in total

- **Personal details**
    o Confirm your full name
    o Date of birth
    o Telephone number
    o Confirm your current address
    o Confirm other recent addresses
    o State whether you have a disability or if you will require any special facilities when attending the Official Receiver's office for interview

- **Asset Details**
    o Is your property owned or rented?
    o If owned, is the property solely owned or jointly owned?

- o   If owned, what do you estimate to be the value of the property?
- o   If owned, what is the outstanding mortgage?
- o   If owned, who is the mortgage lender?
- o   If rented, provide the name and address of the landlord
- o   If other, for example lodgings, provide details
- o   Do you own a motor vehicle?
- o   If yes, what do you estimate to be the value of the vehicle?
- o   If yes, what is the make, model and registration of the vehicle?
- o   If yes, is the vehicle insured?
- o   If yes, where is the location of the vehicle?
- o   If yes, is the vehicle subject to a hire purchase agreement or other finance agreement? If so, provide details.
- o   Do you own premium bonds?
- o   Do you own shares?
- o   Do you own any other assets worth £1,000 or above?
- o   Provide details of your bank accounts.

- **Trading History/employment**
  - o   Are you currently employed/unemployed/self-employed?
  - o   Have you traded at all in the last two years?
  - o   If yes, have you traded as a sole trader or in partnership?
  - o   When did the business cease trading?
  - o   What did the business do?
  - o   What was the trading name?
  - o   What was the trading address?
  - o   Were business premises owned or rented or did you trade from home?
  - o   If business premises were owned, rented, or subject to a lease, provide details.
  - o   Where are the keys to the premises?
  - o   Is there any stock, equipment, or other assets held at the business premises?
  - o   Are contents insured?

- o   Provide details of employees still working
- o   Are the trading records held at the premises? If not, where are they kept?

+ **Partnership Details (additional to above)**
  - o   Provide names and addresses of other partners
  - o   Are any partners also bankrupt?
  - o   Provide Partnership accountant and solicitor details
  - o   What are approximately the total Partnership liabilities?

6. Bankrupt interviewed (if considered necessary)

As the Bankruptcy Order requires Bob to give information about his financial affairs, Bob may be worried about being given the "third degree". However, the Examiner will be happy to deal with Bob's concern as he gathers the information and the feedback is that Bankrupt's are satisfied with this process. Bob is likely to experience the following:

The Examiner first asks Bob if he has any time restrictions and should offer him breaks during the interview. The Examiner should also ask whether Bob has a disability or if he will require any special facilities during the interview. The Examiner then goes on to explain that the purpose of the interview is to identify any assets that Bob may have, to identify who his creditors are, and identify and understand the cause of his bankruptcy.

The Examiner will explain that **Bob's bankruptcy will last for one year from the date of the bankruptcy order.** After exactly one year has passed Bob will be discharged from bankruptcy i.e. the restrictions and obligations explained above will no longer be held against him. Whilst Bob will in effect, once again, be a free agent, he will need to rebuild his credit record and the entries made by the private Credit Reference Agencies will stay on his record for six years.

The Examiner will demystify the process and make sure that Bob fully understands the restrictions and obligations held against him, as explained in the form that Bob should now have signed and returned to the Official Receiver's office. Before starting the interview the Examiner will briefly explain what The Insolvency Service is and its purpose and who the Official Receiver is and what his duties include.

The different titles can be daunting and the Examiner will explain that the Official Receiver may end up as Trustee - the Trustee is responsible for selling assets and making the distribution of funds to creditors. The Creditors can decide to appoint an Insolvency Practitioner as Trustee. If this appointment is made then these responsibilities will be held by the Insolvency Practitioner as Trustee. If no one else is appointed the Official Receiver does it by default.

The Examiner will check Bob has received a copy of the bankruptcy order and the 'guide to bankruptcy'. The 'guide to bankruptcy' is a booklet provided by The Insolvency Service that gives an overview of how bankruptcy works.

As Bob is obliged by The Insolvency Act to answer the questions, if he is not truthful this would be perjury and before the interview gets underway, the Examiner will read to Bob Section 5 of the Perjury Act 1911. The thrust of this legislation is that any documents, answers or sworn declarations must be true to the best of the bankrupt's information knowledge and belief. The issue involves materiality such that to miss out a minor item would be considered understandable whereas forgetting to list a house would not.

At this point, the interview will begin. The purpose of the interview is to identify the cause of financial failure and the Examiner will follow the money. The basis of the interview is to run through the questions and answers that Bob stated in either his statement of affairs (if Bob petitioned for his own bankruptcy) or the bankruptcy questionnaire (if a creditor petitioned for Bob's bankruptcy) and identify how the debts have arisen. Both the 'Statement of Affairs' and the 'Preliminary Information Questionnaire' contain essentially the same questions, but they only describe the end position. Accordingly the Examiner will look at the spending patterns, business and personal losses in the run up to the bankruptcy and see whether this tallies with Bob's explanation.

If Bob brings any books or papers along to the interview with him, he should be handed a receipt from the Examiner for the papers he has handed over. During the interview the Examiner will write a list of what he requires to be delivered to him by Bob at a later date. At the end of the interview Bob will be asked to sign this list. The 'request for further information form' states that Bob will provide the Official Receiver with this requested information within 14 days and likely requests include:

- Bank statements
- Credit card statements
- Copies of payslips
- Trading books and records (if of course Bob traded a business)

During the interview the Examiner will take notes and at the end of the interview the Examiner will ask Bob to read through this statement and to sign it. If Bob cannot read/forgot his glasses and was unable to read the statement, it would be read to him.

For the majority of people this is the end of the interviewing process, but with some of my scenarios the Examiner found that Bob's alter egos were up to misconduct and called them back to respond to his findings (chapters 7 and 8).

7. Trustee appointed

If the bankrupt's assets are of high value, it may be decided to arrange a meeting of Creditors for the appointment of an Insolvency Practitioner as Trustee to deal with the assets appropriately. The timing of the Trustee appointment is down to the urgency. Most appointments will be made after the bankrupt has been interviewed and the appointed Trustee is usually the Official Receiver.

The appointment of a Trustee is a formal process, and the decision is made in accordance as to whether a meeting of creditors is held, and if so, its outcome. This has to be done within 16 weeks, but the Official Receiver aims to do it quicker.

If a meeting of creditors is held:
Once a majority vote has been made by the Creditors (i.e. once more than 50% of creditors agree) the appointment of the chosen Insolvency Practitioner can be made.

If a meeting of creditors is not held:
The Official Receiver automatically becomes Trustee when a 'notice of no meeting' is sent to creditors and the court informing them that it has been decided that no meeting is necessary.

If a bankrupt does not cooperate and attend for interview and there are assets, the Official Receiver will likely hold a meeting of creditors resulting in the appointment of an Insolvency Practitioner as Trustee. Insolvency Practitioners are handsomely paid for their time and significantly more than the Official Receiver, so it would be very foolish not to cooperate if Bob's position was salvageable.

8. Report written and sent to creditors

After the interview the Official Receiver summarises the findings and sends a report to Bob's Creditors. This report will detail Bob's assets and will summarise his total liabilities (total amount owing to creditors). The report will briefly explain the cause of Bob's insolvency and will state (what most creditors are really interested in) whether they are likely to be paid in part or in full (a distribution of funds to creditors).

Once the report to creditors has been sent (usually within one to two weeks from the date of the interview), Bob's creditors will know about the bankruptcy and if appropriate they will be invited to appoint an Insolvency Practitioner to be Trustee to deal with his bankruptcy affairs.

Once the report has been sent to all of Bob's creditors, most will update their records and Bob should no longer be chased for payment by his creditors. If any creditors do continue to chase him for payment it is advisable that Bob first makes sure they are aware of the bankruptcy order and then refers them to the Examiner at The Insolvency Service dealing with his bankruptcy affairs. Mostly the law does not allow a creditor to ignore the process and push for payment, but there are exceptions such as fines and family maintenance where it would be wrong to let Bob walk away.

It is likely that Bob will not be contacted by the Official Receiver's office again, other than perhaps to chase up on documents that he may have agreed to hand in.

9. Internal conduct report prepared by Examiner detailing his recommendation.

The Examiner will now write an internal report, recommending any further action to be taken. If the Examiner is satisfied with the explanations given and the information provided by Bob he may recommend that no further investigation is required and may recommend an early discharge from bankruptcy. If the Examiner had cause to recommend further investigation in his report then his reasons will be reviewed by the Assistant Official Receiver who makes the final decision. The Assistant Official Receiver will state whether he agrees or disagrees with the Examiner's recommendation for either further investigation, or no further investigation and perhaps an early discharge from bankruptcy.

Current insolvency law states that Bob will remain bankrupt for exactly one year. However, it is possible, if the administration is completed quickly and it is decided that there are no further matters that require further investigation, that Bob may obtain an early discharge from bankruptcy. In this instance Bob may only be bankrupt for six or seven months, rather than the full year.

10. Possible further investigation and repercussions of any misconduct found

Matters that may warrant a decision to carry out further investigations are explained in detail in both chapters 7 and 8.

Who will be notified of the bankruptcy?

In addition to the 10 steps listed above, it is important to understand who else will be notified of the bankruptcy order.

Shortly after the order has been made the details of Bob's bankruptcy will be advertised in a local newspaper, in the London Gazette and on a public register which is available at www.insolvency.gov.uk. The advertisement will set out Bob's name, whether he is employed, details of any trading and past and present addresses e.g.

Bob Smith trading as Smith and Son Builders, of 10 Eagle Close, Broke Town, lately of 12 Hawk Street, Spendalot, formerly of 22 Kestrel Drive, Thrifty Town.

The Examiner assigned for a bankruptcy case will send letters out to various parties, to both notify them of the bankruptcy order and to request further information. This is to minimise the risk that assets or records are lost whether by accident or design. Such parties contacted are in particular:

- Bank

- Landlord (if property rented)

- Mortgage lender (if property owned)

- Accountant (if an accountant has acted on behalf of the bankrupt)

- Solicitor (if a solicitor has acted on behalf of the bankrupt)

- Finance company (if property such as a vehicle is owned on Hire Purchase)

- Credit card/loan companies

The Official Receiver's duty to request such information is set out in the **Insolvency Act 1986:**

Section 289 of the Insolvency Act 1986 states that the Official Receiver has a statutory duty to investigate the financial affairs of a bankrupt.

The Data Protection Act will not prevent the Official Receiver from obtaining such information as Section 31 of The Data Protection Act allows people to provide information to the Official Receiver.

Section 366 of the Insolvency Act 1986 allows the Official Receiver to ask the court to summon any person to appear at court that may hold information regarding the bankrupt's financial affairs. The court may require any such person to submit an affidavit to the court containing an account of his dealings with the bankrupt or to produce any documents in his possession or under his control relating to the bankrupt or the bankrupt's dealings, affairs or property.

Chapter 6

Bankruptcy – How does it work?

Bob has just been made bankrupt and he's heard stories that bailiffs turn up and take everything away. Let me dispel those myths and clarify what he is likely to be able to keep and what he is likely to lose.

Now that Bob has been made bankrupt, most assets belonging to him will now be under the control of the bankruptcy. In pure legal terms the assets originally fall under the control of the Official Receiver as "Receiver and Manager". He wears that hat until a decision has been made on a "Trustee" in bankruptcy. Whilst Receiver and Manager the assets are technically still Bob's – but he is bound by law to hand control to the Official Receiver. As soon as either the Official Receiver or the Insolvency Practitioner is appointed Trustee, the assets vest in the Trustee in bankruptcy – when the assets vest they cease to be Bob's and are owned by the Trustee.

Who is the "Trustee"?

The Trustee is the person who deals with the assets and pays the creditors.

The Trustee in bankruptcy is likely to be the Official Receiver of the local area in which Bob lives. However an Insolvency Practitioner may act as Trustee of Bob's bankruptcy estate. Insolvency Practitioners hold formal insolvency qualifications and must be insured to act; accordingly they charge substantially more than the Official Receiver for the work that they do.

The Trustee will be responsible for protecting any assets Bob owns, selling assets and distributing monies evenly between creditors. The distribution will be made on a pro-rata basis.

The decision to appoint an Insolvency Practitioner as Trustee of a bankruptcy estate other than the Official Receiver is usually due to there being a high value of assets, continuing business or a complex asset owned by the bankrupt such as a trading commercial property, with a significant amount of stock or machinery. This effectively means that once appointed all responsibilities concerning assets would then be dealt with by the Insolvency Practitioner as Trustee rather than the Official Receiver.

Insolvency Practitioner (IP) – a good idea?

As with most decisions it depends on the circumstances. If Bob were solvent (his assets exceeded his creditors), it would be a balancing exercise.

If Bob has a high value of assets, the Official Receiver or Bob's creditors may look to appoint an Insolvency Practitioner as Trustee in bankruptcy. The Official Receiver will however continue to deal with investigation matters in the bankruptcy.

If Bob is trading and would lose a lot of money if trading stops then unless he can get the bankruptcy cancelled (annulled) in days, only an Insolvency Practitioner has the power to trade the business. There Bob may weigh that the extra cost of the Insolvency Practitioner is more than offset by not having to close his business for a time.

If Bob is merely employed and can raise funds quickly from family or friends then he can explore other options such as how to get his bankruptcy annulled. Bob needs to ask how much the Official Receiver, Solicitor or Insolvency Practitioner will cost in what he proposes. Indeed it may not even be cost effective to employ a solicitor (annulment is explained in full in chapter 9).

If Bob were solvent, he should not bury his head in the sand and ignore the threat of bankruptcy. If he did an Insolvency Practitioner would be appointed and this would incur further costs, usually on a time and charge rate basis and costs could go through the roof. If Bob contacted the Official Receiver immediately and took steps to apply for an annulment the Official Receiver would hold onto the case for a reasonable time and would not seek the immediate appointment of an Insolvency Practitioner as Trustee.

As all bankruptcies are advertised, if Bob was in a position to apply for annulment, he could also ask the court for a stay of advertisement which would prevent the advertisement from going out. **For further information on the possibility of having a bankruptcy annulled (cancelled) see chapter 9.**

So what will be considered as an asset and what will happen to these assets?

An asset is anything that Bob owns that has a value. This can range from anything such as a car, to an intangible (non-physical asset) such as goodwill in a business.

Under Section 282 of the Insolvency Act certain assets are exempt from bankruptcy and Bob will be allowed to retain these assets:

A vehicle and other items will be exempt from the bankruptcy proceedings if required for Bob's employment, business or vocation. Property required for domestic needs such as clothing, bedding, furniture, and household equipment will also be exempt.

Motor Vehicle

Bob's motor vehicle will be exempt from the bankruptcy proceedings if it is required for work purposes or if Bob is currently unemployed but requires the vehicle for seeking work and will then require the vehicle once he has found new employment. The rules are quite strict and there are few other circumstances that allow for a vehicle to be exempt from the proceedings.

The exemption of a motor vehicle can fall under the domestic needs provisions in exceptional circumstances. In order for the Trustee to exempt a vehicle under this section the bankrupt will have to provide evidence to the Trustee that no practical alternative exists such as public transport. Possible circumstances are where the bankrupt is disabled and requires the vehicle for his mobility, or if the vehicle is required for taking children to school. However, the Trustee must be convinced that no practical alternative for transport exists.

Even if Bob's vehicle is required for travelling to and from work, it would not necessarily be safe to immediately assume that he would keep the vehicle. When agreeing a vehicle is exempt, the Trustee will consider the value of the vehicle. With few exceptions, the Official Receiver applies a capped value of £2,000. So if Bob owned a Rolls Royce worth well above the capped amount of £2,000 then the vehicle would have to be realised (sold) and £2,000 from the proceeds of this sale would be returned to Bob in order to purchase a vehicle that could get him to and from work. The legislation is strict in this respect and if Bob claims the vehicle is exempt then the Trustee must act within 42 days from the date of the claim otherwise Bob will be allowed to keep the Rolls!

The purpose of this procedure is to strike the right balance between being fair to Bob and acting in the best interests of Bob's Creditors. Few would consider it fair for Bob to retain a vehicle worth say £10,000, probably paid for using an unsecured loan, when a cheaper car would transport him adequately. It is considered fair to both Bob and his creditors to allow the retention of a motor vehicle if required, as not only will any surplus value (amount above the £2,000 cap) be realised to contribute to a distribution of funds to his creditors, but it will also allow Bob to work and make contributions into the bankruptcy. These contributions may very well amount to more than the value of Bob's vehicle.

Regarding the exemption of vehicles, the £2,000 cap is treated as a guideline rather than an exact figure. If Bob had an old Rolls worth £10,000 used to earn an income from wedding hire, then if he made income contributions it may be appropriate to accept the claim that the vehicle was exempt and should not be replaced. If the vehicle was estimated to realise marginally more, for example £2,300, the costs of dealing with any realisation may make it practical to merely accept that the whole vehicle be exempt from the bankruptcy proceedings.

If Bob were to disagree with the decision of the Trustee he could refer the matter to the Court and they would make the final decision.

If Bob's vehicle is to be sold, can he buy it back from the Trustee in bankruptcy?

If the vehicle is to be sold and Bob wishes to retain it, then a friend or relative may put in an offer for the surplus value (amount above the £2,000 cap). However, the Official Receiver (if Trustee) will need to check that the offer is fair. For example, if the vehicle had been valued by an agent acting for the Official Receiver at £3,500 and Bob's friend or relative was willing to put in an offer for the £1,500 surplus value on the vehicle, then this may be accepted. This also applies to any other asset that may be realised for the purposes of the bankruptcy and often arises with items of sentimental value.

For example:
Bob has a private number plate on his motor vehicle of which he is very fond. After the Official Receiver's agent has valued the registration plate, Bess (Bob's Extremely Supportive Spouse) puts in a realistic offer for the asset. This was purchased by the third party (Bess) and Bob was therefore able to retain possession of the asset. It is to be hoped he doesn't fall out with Bess as she now owns the registration plate and could sell it on should she so wish.

If a vehicle is not an exempt asset in bankruptcy, then the Trustee must dispose of the vehicle, even if it has to be scrapped. In these circumstances it can cost more in agent fees to dispose of the asset than the realisable value (sale value) of the car, but an un-roadworthy or un-insured car can do a lot of harm and the Trustee can not just ignore it. Therefore if Bob has a motor vehicle that is worth approximately £200 and Bob is unemployed, the vehicle must be disposed of (as it is not required for work purposes). If a third party was to put in a minimal offer of say £50, it will almost certainly be accepted by the Trustee in bankruptcy as it will in effect be a cost saving exercise.

> If a third party is going to put in an offer for an asset it is worth taking consideration into how much should be offered.

It is important to note that Bob can put in an offer to retain an asset himself, but only from any surplus income (See income payment agreements explained later in this chapter as to how this is calculated) – as any other money/asset owned by Bob is a bankruptcy asset. Therefore it is probable that a third party will have to put in the offer. This could perhaps be Bess or another relative or friend who has not been made bankrupt.

If an Insolvency Practitioner (IP) is appointed as Trustee, then Bob would need to discuss how best to deal with the asset with the IP, as the IP's procedure is likely to differ to that of the Official Receiver's.

Will Bob lose his pension?

Most pension policies (although not all) are exempt from bankruptcy proceedings, and cannot be realised as a bankruptcy asset. If Bob had been concerned as to whether the Trustee could take his pension, he could have checked with his pension company whether the scheme was exempt from bankruptcy proceedings; he didn't and the Trustee checked and confirmed it was his to keep.

Will Bob's home be inspected?

It is very rare for the Official Receiver to carry out an inspection of a property. In the past, when bankruptcies were not nearly so high in number, each and every bankruptcy would have a property inspection to see if there were any assets to be recovered and items such as video recorders would be considered luxuries and sold. Now bankruptcies are so frequent and consumer goods realise so little, that it is simply not cost effective to visit every bankrupt. Therefore, unless the Official Receiver has very good cause to carry out an inspection, he won't. If an Insolvency Practitioner is appointed as Trustee it is more likely that an inspection will take place. However, in the majority of bankruptcy cases, the Official Receiver will be appointed as Trustee.

As property inspections are generally not carried out, if Bob were a dishonest chap and did not disclose certain assets to the Official Receiver there is a chance that the Official Receiver wouldn't find out. If, for example, Bob owned a painting worth £10,000 and did not disclose this asset to the Official Receiver either in his statement of affairs, questionnaire, or interview, then the Official Receiver may have no way of immediately knowing. Whilst the Official Receiver relies to a large degree upon Bob (the bankrupt) being honest, if he is not then information from creditors and whistle blowers would leave him in difficulty. Indeed, in this example it would likely be easy to show his ownership just by recovering his insurance policy, which often lists valuables. I do not advocate that Bob or any other person going bankrupt should be dishonest, that would be in contravention of his disclosure obligations under The Insolvency Act and the Perjury Act and if Bob were found to have been dishonest **there may be serious repercussions**, as explained further in chapters 7 and 8.

Bob owns his home. Will it be sold?

If Bob had a house in his own name then, with few exceptions, whatever the Trustee realises is used to pay creditors. If a property is jointly owned, then it is the share of the property owned by Bob that would be considered as a bankruptcy asset. Most house owners have secured borrowing and the Trustee has to pay this first and the difference is called equity – the equity is the asset and Bob's equity will be realised if there is enough to make it worth while; Realising equity can take many forms, selling on the open market, taking a charge or selling to a spouse or friend. Indeed Bob could buy the equity back once he obtained his discharge. Therefore in the following example:

Bob jointly owns the following property with his wife Bess;

Detail	**Value**
House value:	
12 Common Drive, Standard Town	£170,000
Less secured debts:	
Outstanding mortgage	(£70,000)
Other secured charges	(£10,000)
Equity in property	£90,000
Bob's share in equity (50%)	**£45,000**

> The equity is the value in the property less any secured debts such as a mortgage. In other words the equity is the amount that will be received after the property has been sold and all relating charges have been paid off.

In the above example Bob's share of the equity in the property is £45,000; this will form an asset in the bankruptcy. The joint owner in the property (Bess) or any other relative or friend will have the opportunity to purchase Bob's beneficial share in the property. If so, this would eliminate the

Trustee's interest in the property. Otherwise, it is likely the property will be sold to realise the bankruptcy asset.

It is worth noting the following:
With Bob's home he has a right of occupation for up to a year, so the Trustee cannot sell it until that time has passed. Also if the Trustee does not realise the property within three years Bob automatically gets his interest back. Whilst Bob has some time to decide how he wants to deal with the house it is worth remembering that house prices can go up or down and he should take this into account as well as the ability to keep up with mortgage repayments.

If Bess wanted to purchase Bob's share in the property she would have to talk to the Trustee.

If Official Receiver is appointed as Trustee of Bob's bankruptcy estate:

The Official Receiver follows the same procedure throughout the country. Bess must first obtain an up to date professional valuation of the property together with details of all mortgages and charges secured against the property which she passes to the Official Receiver. On top of this the Official Receiver will have to be paid £211 in advance of the transaction to cover solicitor's costs. A value will have to then be agreed between the two parties (Bess and the Official Receiver).

If there was a nil or negative equity in the property, Bess may still wish to purchase Bob's share (beneficial interest) in the equity. If she chose to do this, Bess would be required to pay £1 to the Official Receiver for the interest in the property in addition to the £211 solicitor's costs. It is worth noting in this situation that if Bess is named on the mortgage, she is not taking on any further debt as the mortgage company can already chase her to pay the entire mortgage.

If an Insolvency Practitioner (IP) is appointed as Trustee of Bob's bankruptcy estate:

There are many different IPs with differing procedures and Bess would have to contact the Insolvency Practitioner to find out how best to purchase the beneficial interest from the IP.

What would be the advantage in purchasing a nil or negative equity in the property?

A clear advantage is that this preserves Bob's home and his family will not have to uproot. The advantage to Bess is that she already has to pay the mortgage and by buying out Bob's interest she protects herself from the house having to be sold by the Trustee in the future should there be an increase in house prices.

If there is a nil or negative equity in the property (i.e. secured charges against the property such as the mortgage exceeds the value of the property) it will be placed on a "long term realisations register" and monitored during the three years following the date of the bankruptcy order. If during this time there is a realisable equity in the property, the Trustee will look to realise this asset. There would be some change in the equity over this time as mortgage payments would have been paid since the date of the bankruptcy order, reducing the mortgage; also house prices may have changed. In recent years the expectation has been that house price rises will automatically result in a rise in equity, but that depends on keeping the mortgage up to date and, as has been seen in 2008, there is no guarantee that prices ever continue to rise indefinitely.

It is therefore possible that a nil or negative equity could have become a positive equity in this time. Although a bankruptcy only lasts for one year or indeed a shorter period if an early discharge is obtained, **the property can still be realised within three years of the bankruptcy order.**

If it were a friend or relative buying the equity there is significant advantage to buying the "beneficial interest" (or ultimate sale proceeds), which is different to the "legal interest" (the person named at the Land Registry and on the mortgage). You get an asset with few risks, as should it be repossessed they are not named on the mortgage and any shortfall would be a claim against Bob's bankruptcy, although if Bob "novates" by signing mortgage documents after bankruptcy he may be liable again.

For these reasons it may very well be worth Bess a friend or relative purchasing the nil/negative share in the property for the meagre sum of £1 (plus the additional £211). However, the law in this area is particularly unforgiving and it is not DIY territory; you need legal advice if you are to ensure that you obtain the benefits and minimise the risks. Once a third party purchases this interest from the Trustee, it takes the Trustee out of the equation.

> It is the beneficial interest that will be purchased. The proprietors (home owners) names registered against the property (in this case Bob and his wife) will remain unchanged. The significant factor is that Bob's wife will have purchased Bob's beneficial interest in the property.

Can the Trustee claim Registered Assets?

A common mistake that people make is the assumption that if a name is registered against an asset such as a house or a car then the asset automatically belongs to that person.

For example, Bob may claim that the vehicle he drives belongs to his wife and therefore is not a bankruptcy asset. If Bob's reasoning behind this is because the vehicle has been registered in his wife's name, Bob would be incorrect to believe that this fact alone means that the vehicle belongs to his wife and not him.

It is not the registered name that determines the ownership of the car. If Bob purchased the vehicle, was the only person that drove the vehicle and paid for the fuel, maintenance and insurance on the vehicle; if the only thing that tied the vehicle to his wife was the fact that it was registered in her name, then the financial interest in the vehicle would be considered to belong to Bob. Also, if this was done on purpose to keep the asset out of the bankruptcy there would be serious consequences (see chapters 7 and 8).

Will Bob lose the money in his bank account?

If there is a credit balance in Bob's bank account, this will form an asset in the bankruptcy. The Trustee will realise this amount, however the Trustee may release any amount that is considered to represent Bob's monthly income. After all Bob needs money to live on and payments from income should be formalised by way of an income payments agreement or order.

Following the bankruptcy order, all of Bob's bank accounts will be frozen. If an account is used for Bob's monthly income and expenditure, it is likely the Trustee will inform the bank that he is happy for Bob to continue using this account and the decision to allow Bob to continue using this account is down to the bank's own discretion. If the bank does not wish to allow Bob to continue banking with them then they are perfectly within their rights to close his account.

Following the bankruptcy order, there is nothing to stop Bob from opening a new bank account with someone else; however he should inform the bank that he is subject to a bankruptcy order. It is unlikely that a bank will allow Bob an overdraft facility whilst subject to a bankruptcy order, and if Bob obtained an overdraft facility of more than £500 without first informing the bank that he is subject to a bankruptcy order he would be committing a criminal offence.

What happens to Assets subject to Hire Purchase?

There are a range of legal agreements in which Bob could get an asset on finance where it wasn't actually his until he made the final payment. Whilst Hire Purchase is just one such agreement they are often collectively referred to using this term.

If Bob has a vehicle under a hire purchase agreement, the agreement is likely to say they are entitled to take it back if he is made bankrupt. However the hire purchase company is likely to be willing to continue the agreement regardless of Bob's bankruptcy. This is because it is generally in the hire purchase company's interest to continue the agreement. For example:

Detail	Value
Ford Focus (Bob's car)	£3,000
Outstanding finance	£5,000
Shortfall	(£2,000)

In the above case if the hire purchase company repossessed Bob's vehicle they would lose £2,000, being the amount they are still owed by Bob after the car is sold. This would then be included as a bankruptcy debt, but in most cases this would mean that the hire purchase company is unlikely to receive all (if any) of its money back. Therefore hire purchase companies are generally happy to continue the agreement in the hope of receiving full payment.

Will the Trustee take Bob's other assets?

The items Bob needs for his normal domestic needs are exempt by law and the Trustee cannot sell them (it is of interest that these goods are not even available to a bailiff were Bob not bankrupt). Accordingly, general household goods of a reasonable value are unlikely to be sold by the Trustee for the purposes of the bankruptcy estate. General household goods are the obvious items, such as beds, sofa and chairs, dining room table, television, etc. Common sense prevails when considering the value of such items. For example, if Bob owned a bog standard television, this would not be realised as a bankruptcy asset. However, if Bob owned a 50" Plasma screen television, this has a significant value and would be considered to be an unnecessary household item that would accordingly not be exempt and as such would form a bankruptcy asset.

If Bob has a business or is self employed and requires his tools for his trade, he can claim these are exempt from the proceedings as they are required if he is to continue his profession. Again the value of these tools must be taken into consideration e.g. If Bob had a haulage business and tried to claim a £50,000 lorry as exempt property, at best he should expect that the lorry is sold and a cheap replacement bought.

Income Payment Agreements and Orders (IPAs and IPOs)

We must not forget Bob's creditors have rights and the purpose of an IPA is that if Bob can afford to contribute a percentage of his income each month into the bankruptcy estate then he should. This is obviously another method of collecting funds to pay the bankruptcy creditors some or all of what they are owed. In most bankruptcies the Official Receiver is Trustee and the following outlines the Official Receiver's approach. If an Insolvency Practitioner is appointed as Trustee there are likely to be variations on this procedure.

Following the IPA procedure:
An IPA will be calculated on the basis of Bob's monthly income after deducting his reasonable monthly expenditure. This calculation will be based upon details that Bob will have stated in either his 'Statement of Affairs' if Bob petitioned for his own bankruptcy or the 'Preliminary Information Questionnaire' (Form PIQB) if a creditor petitioned for Bob's bankruptcy. Both forms contain a section for the bankrupt to complete his monthly income and expenditure details. From this information it is decided by the Official Receiver whether he can afford to contribute towards the bankruptcy from his income.

Income Payment Agreements (IPAs) are set for a fixed term of 36 months. Therefore the agreement will continue beyond the date that Bob will be discharged from his bankruptcy.

If it is decided that there is no scope for an IPA, it may be that Bob will be sent an income/expenditure form to complete at a later date. The period of the IPA is thirty six months, and it starts when Bob and the Official Receiver sign the agreement.

How is the IPA calculated?

If, for example, Bob's income after tax is £1,200 and his essential monthly outgoings amount to £1,000, then the monthly surplus income in this instance would be £200. Bob would be expected to pay a percentage of this surplus income into the bankruptcy each month for a period of thirty six months. In this instance he would be expected to pay £100 towards the bankruptcy each month. This is based on a calculation of a contributory payment of 50% of surplus earnings.

The IPA contribution is not calculated on a fixed percentage. The level of the surplus income determines the percentage to be used when calculating the monthly contribution to be paid by the bankrupt. Please see the following table:

IPA table

All figures are on a monthly basis

Surplus income £	Amount to be paid £	% of disposable income
0	0	0
50	0	0
60	0	0
70	0	0
80	0	0
90	0	0
100	50	50
110	55	50
120	60	50
130	65	50
140	70	50
150	75	50
160	80	50
170	85	50
180	90	50
190	95	50
200	100	50
210	105	50
220	110	50
230	115	50
240	120	50
250	150	60
260	156	60
270	162	60
280	168	60
290	174	60
300	180	60
310	186	60

320	192	60
330	198	60
340	204	60
350	231	66
360	238	66
370	244	66
380	251	66
390	257	66
400	264	66
410	271	66
420	277	66
430	284	66
440	290	66
450	297	66
460	304	66
470	310	66
480	317	66
490	323	66
500	350	70
510	357	70
520	364	70
530	371	70
540	378	70
550	385	70

The maximum contribution that can be paid is 70%.

Not all expenditure will be accepted by the Official Receiver. For example tobacco would not be considered as essential monthly expenditure. The idea is that the percentage of the "surplus" earnings that Bob retains can be spent by him as he wishes. Therefore if for example Bob wishes to purchase cigarettes this would have to be purchased from his share of the surplus earnings.

In the following further examples the calculation has been split to show how Bob may list his expenditure (shown on the left) and how the Examiner/Official Receiver may review the expenditure (shown on the right hand side of the table).

Example 1

Bob's Income against expenditure

Expenditure listed as per bankrupt		Expenditure reviewed by Official Receiver	
Outgoings		**Outgoings**	
Mortgage/Rent	600	Mortgage/Rent	600
Housekeeping	300	Housekeeping	300
Gas, Elec, Heating	200	Gas, Elec, Heating	100
Water	50	Water	50
Telephone Charges	50	Telephone Charges	50
Travel to/from work	100	Travel to/from work	100
Clothing	90	Clothing	40
Fines/Maintenance	150	Fines/Maintenance	150
Council Tax	112	Council Tax	112
Other Essential payments:		*Other Essential payments:*	
Car Insurance	*40*	*Car Insurance*	*40*
TV Licence	*11*	*TV Licence*	*11*
Tobacco	*50*	*Tobacco*	*0*
Social events	*50*	*Social events*	*0*
Other Essential payments	151	Other Essential payments	51
Total Outgoings	**1,803**	**Total Outgoings**	**1,553**
Income		**Income**	
Monthly take home pay	1,820	Monthly take home pay	1,820
Other household income	0	Other household income	0
Total Income	**1,820**	**Total Income**	**1,820**
Surplus monthly income	**17**	Surplus monthly income	**267**
Suggested monthly IPA	0	Suggested monthly IPA	156

As can be seen in the example above, Bob has listed what he considers to be his monthly income and expenditure: His monthly income after tax is £1,820, Bob considers his essential monthly outgoings to be £1,803 and this leaves Bob with a surplus income of just £17 per month. As shown in the IPA table, a surplus income of under £100 per month does not warrant a monthly IPA contribution; therefore if the Examiner/Official Receiver agrees to the information stated by Bob, he would not be expected to make monthly contributions towards his bankruptcy.

On the right hand side of the above example, the Examiner/Official Receiver has reviewed this information and has adjusted some of the figures to what he believes would be a reasonable monthly expenditure. As can be seen above, tobacco and social events have been removed completely as the Official Receiver does not agree that these are "essential expenditure".

Some expenditure stated by Bob has been reduced. E.g. The Examiner does not believe that Bob requires £90 per month for clothing and his allowance has been reduced to £40 per month.

As can be seen in the right hand side of the above table, following adjustments made to the IPA form, the monthly surplus income of Bob is now stated as being £267. Following the IPA table it can be seen that this sum warrants an IPA calculation based on the percentage of 60% of the surplus income and the monthly IPA contribution to be paid by Bob has therefore been calculated at £156.

The Examiner/Official Receiver may request further information regarding some of the expenditure that Bob has stated, such as the £150 per month paid in maintenance for his child. It is possible the Official Receiver may ask for proof of this or any other monthly expenditure. If employed, the Official Receiver will require Bob to provide copies of payslips to provide evidence of his monthly income. If Bob is to continue in self employment Bob will be required to prove his monthly business income and expenditure.

Example 2

If there is another household income, this will also be considered when calculating Bob's IPA. Some think this is unfair from a privacy perspective; the other people contributing to the household income are not bankrupt and why should their affairs be considered? The Official Receiver only intends to review Bob's sole income and sole expenditure, but to do so he needs to eliminate the other household members' expenditure from the household expenditure listed by Bob.

In short, Bob's income and expenditure is effectively all that is being considered to calculate the IPA, however in order to make this calculation it is necessary to know what the total household income is, which can be explained in the following example:

Book of Bankruptcy: The simple guide to bankruptcy and other remedies to debt

Expenditure listed as per bankrupt			Expenditure reviewed by Official Receiver		
Outgoings			**Outgoings**		
Mortgage/Rent		550	Mortgage/Rent		550
Housekeeping		280	Housekeeping		280
Gas, Elec, Heating		60	Gas, Elec, Heating		60
Water		40	Water		40
Telephone Charges		40	Telephone Charges		40
Travel to/from work		20	Travel to/from work		20
Clothing		40	Clothing		40
Fines/Maintenance		0	Fines/Maintenance		0
Council Tax		90	Council Tax		90
Other Essential payments:			*Other Essential payments:*		
Car Insurance	25		Car Insurance	25	
TV Licence	*11*		TV Licence	*11*	
Other Essential payments		36	Other Essential payments		36
Total Outgoings		**1,156**	Total Outgoings		**1,156**
Income			**Income**		
Monthly take home pay		1,100	Monthly take home pay		1,100
Other household income		600	Other household income		600
Total Income		**1,700**	Total Income		**1,700**
Surplus monthly income		Nil	Surplus monthly income		SEE BELOW
Suggested monthly IPA		Nil	Suggested monthly IPA		SEE BELOW

As can be seen in the above example, the Official Receiver has made no changes to Bob's monthly outgoings as they all appear reasonable.

Bob's income in this example is £1,100 per month; his outgoings are £1,156 per month. Therefore if you ignore the other householder, Bob's income less expenditure does not appear to generate a surplus income and it therefore would not seem reasonable for Bob to contribute a monthly payment from his income towards the bankruptcy.

However, Bob has stated that his wife is taking home £600 per month in salary and the total household income is £1,700 per month being Bob's monthly salary of £1,100 and his wife's salary of £600 per month. Some of Bob's expenditure listed above would be joint household expenditure such as mortgage/rent for the family home. It would clearly be unreasonable to expect Bob to pay all the household expenditure when his wife is also earning and should therefore be contributing towards the household expenditure. To be fair to Bob's creditors it is therefore necessary to revise Bob's expenditure so that his income is offset against his sole expenditure.

55

On the basis that total household income is £1,700 per month, Bob's salary amounts to 65% of £1,700. Following is a calculation of Bob's expenditure measured proportionately to his income, as per the percentage calculated at 65%. However, where an expense is solely attributable to Bob's income, such as his costs for travelling to and from work, it is not adjusted.

Revised Expenditure

Outgoings			100% Bob's expenditure
Mortgage/Rent		356	No
Housekeeping		181	No
Gas, Elec, Heating		39	No
Water		26	No
Telephone Charges		26	No
Travel to/from work		20	Yes
Clothing		40	Yes
Fines/Maintenance		0	No
Council Tax		58	No
Car Insurance	25		Yes
TV Licence	7		No
Other Essential payments		32	
Total Outgoings		**778**	
Surplus monthly income		322	
Suggested monthly IPA		192	

As you can see above, the items marked "No" are monthly outgoings shared by the household and these outgoings have been reduced by (in this example) 65%; The items marked "Yes" are Bob's sole responsibility and have remained at the full expenditure value as listed in the first table. Therefore the above revised monthly expenditure relates entirely to Bob's sole income.

The monthly surplus income has been calculated as Bob's sole income being £1,100 per month less the monthly expenditure that can be directly linked to his income, being the revised 'total outgoings' sum of £778 per month. As can be seen from the IPA table, Bob's surplus £322 income creates a monthly IPA contribution of 60% amounting to £192.

No two households are the same and two apparently similar households' expenditure may vary widely due to factors such as medical dietary requirements or to the income earners having to travel further to work. Accordingly, income payment agreements vary widely from case to case. There can not be a set guideline as to how much a bankrupt is allowed for household expenditure, for travel expenses etc. The allowances given will be based on the Examiner's own judgement. IPAs are therefore open to negotiation.

Income Payments Orders

If the bankrupt cannot agree an amount with the Examiner and feels that their allowances are unrealistic, they can talk to the Official Receiver who will be happy to provide the official guidelines (which are published on The Insolvency Services website www.insolvency.gov.uk). If after discussion the matter still can not be resolved, the Official Receiver will likely refer the matter to the court and seek a formal order. The bankrupt can accordingly make representations to the judge who will make a decision based on what the court considers fair.

No Tax (NT) coding

Once a bankruptcy order is made the peculiarities of the tax system are such that HM Revenue & Customs (HMRC) will lodge a claim in the bankruptcy for the tax due up until the next 5 April (end of financial tax year) which followed the bankruptcy order. If a bankrupt is employed then he will stop making income tax payments under the pay as you earn scheme and they will not start again until the next 6 April. Therefore during this period up until the end of the current tax year, the bankrupt's income will effectively increase by the amount he pays in tax each month.

This tax is a claim in the bankruptcy and it follows that a bankrupt should not keep the extra in his wage packet as a result of this quirk of the tax system. The Official Receiver accordingly uses the IPA process to collect in an amount equivalent to the bankrupt's monthly tax contributions that are no longer to be paid.

If Bob is employed and pays for example £300 per month in tax, then the Official Receiver will instruct HM Revenue & Customs that the bankruptcy order has been made and they will alter his tax code to NT which will in turn stop the deductions.

Once the NT tax code is in place, Bob's income will increase by the value of tax he normally pays each month from his salary. The Official Receiver will then seek to gain an agreement with Bob through an IPA. This agreement is that the amount Bob would normally pay in tax, he will instead pay towards his bankruptcy estate.

The issue whilst peculiar is financially neutral as far as Bob is concerned as his monthly income will not be affected, as what he would normally be paying in tax is instead being paid to the bankruptcy estate.

If Bob can contribute a percentage of surplus income into the bankruptcy as explained above, then the NT coding is applied in addition as part of the IPA agreement. If it is decided that Bob cannot afford to contribute a percentage of surplus earnings each month, but he is paying tax as an employee, then an IPA will be set for the NT coding alone.

It is worth noting that although the IPA with regard to surplus income is agreed for a set period of thirty six months, the NT coding element is only set until the end of the tax year following the bankruptcy order, being the next 5 April. If when the IPA is being considered it is nearing the end of the current tax year, the collection costs may outweigh any benefit; in such instances the Official Receiver may decide that it is not worthwhile setting up the NT element of an IPA agreement and the bankrupt will keep the extra income (being the unpaid tax contributions created from the NT coding).

Changes in any IPA/IPO

In the period until Bob gets his discharge from bankruptcy he must inform the Official Receiver of any change to his income. If Bob were to receive a pay rise, this may affect the amount to be contributed each month. However Bob is under no obligation to inform the Official Receiver of any change in income once discharged from bankruptcy and even if his income was to dramatically increase he would continue to pay the amount agreed. However, should his income fall, the Official Receiver is likely to agree to either an adjustment to the agreed payment or a suspension in the payment for a period of time.

If Bob refuses to sign to an IPA then the Official Receiver can seek an Income payments order (IPO) from the court. Alternatively, if the issue regards a refusal to provide evidence of the income and expenditure, it will be considered that Bob has not cooperated and the Official Receiver can seek a suspension of Bob's discharge from the court. Bob's discharge from bankruptcy could then be suspended until Bob cooperates with the Official Receiver and indefinitely if there is a complete failure to cooperate.

Chapter 7

Bankruptcy – Sorting the sheep from the goats

Discharge

As explained earlier, bankruptcy lasts for exactly one year from the bankruptcy order.

If Bob had a bankruptcy order made against him on 30 December 2008, under the current insolvency law, Bob will be 'discharged' from bankruptcy on 30 December 2009. However, there are several different circumstances that can affect the period/restrictions of Bob's bankruptcy.

Early discharge

If Bob attends the Official Receiver's office for interview and fully cooperates with the proceedings, once the Official Receiver is satisfied that there are no matters that warrant further investigation he may receive an early discharge. If Bob's case were routine he would likely be discharged 6 to 7 months after the bankruptcy order rather than the usual year.

Public Examination/Suspension of discharge

If Bob thought he could avoid investigation and any consequences of misconduct by failing to attend the Official Receiver's office for interview he would be mistaken and the consequences of attempting to evade responsibility could be worse than facing the music.

The Official Receiver would give Bob a reasonable amount of time to cooperate, but if he did not the Official Receiver would report the matter to the court and ask that Bob be summoned to court. Whether the Official Receiver would seek a Public Examination or suspension of discharge would depend on the nature of Bob's non-cooperation. If Bob continually failed to attend for interview or answer questions, it is probable that he would be publicly examined at court. If he refused to submit documents or hand over assets, it is likely that the application would be for the suspension of Bob's discharge. The outcome of the hearing will turn on Bob's subsequent conduct.

If he fails to attend a hearing for his public examination, the Official Receiver will likely make an immediate application to suspend his discharge – that will extend the obligations and restrictions of bankruptcy until he cooperates and if he fails to cooperate that may in practical terms be indefinitely.

If Bob's discharge were suspended then it is entirely down to Bob to cooperate and ensure that the discharge period starts to run again. If in the future, Bob cooperated and his suspension was lifted, the remaining period of Bob's bankruptcy would have to run in order to be discharged. For example, if Bob's discharge from bankruptcy was suspended 7 months in, then if in say two years time Bob cooperated and his suspension were lifted, the remaining 5 months of Bob's bankruptcy would have to run before he received his discharge from bankruptcy.

What is a suspension of discharge?

To understand the concept of discharge you must first understand the restrictions and obligations of bankruptcy which I outlined in chapter 5. Bankruptcy law provides a series of restrictions and obligations until "discharge". This is normally one year, but if that period is suspended it will be longer.

The obligations allow the Trustee to claim assets that the bankrupt acquires after the date of the bankruptcy order, such as an inheritance or win on the national lottery. The principle restrictions are that you can not:

- get more than £500 credit or trade using a name other than those in the advertised bankruptcy description unless you first disclose your status (i.e. bankrupt or subject to a bankruptcy restrictions order or undertaking);

- act in the management of a company without court permission.

If, for example, regarding Bob's bankruptcy a suspension of discharge had been ordered, then Bob will remain bankrupt until the Official Receiver is satisfied that Bob has fully cooperated with the bankruptcy proceedings. Once Bob cooperates the Official Receiver has only to file a report to that effect and the period starts to run again.

The more common causes resulting in one of these hearings are set out below and most operate on a "three strikes and you're out basis" i.e. if you fail to respond to three requests to deliver up items or explanations the Official Receiver will seek to enforce cooperation or sanction:

1. *Failing to attend for interview/complete bankruptcy questionnaire*

    If Bob fails to fully cooperate, be it either failing to send in the completed questionnaire or failing to attend for interview (or both), this could ultimately result in a suspension of discharge.

The Official Receiver will first send the original appointment letter to Bob arranging a date for interview and requesting he complete and return the questionnaire. If Bob fails to cooperate he will be sent a second letter arranging a further interview appointment and reminding Bob to complete the questionnaire. If Bob again fails to cooperate he will be sent a third and final letter arranging a further appointment to attend the Official Receiver's office for interview and again requesting the completed questionnaire. This final appointment letter will state that if Bob fails to cooperate the Official Receiver may apply to the court for a Public Examination or a Suspension of Discharge. If Bob fails to attend the hearing Bob may be liable to arrest.

> If you are unable to attend the Official Receiver's office for whatever reason, make sure you call the office stating that you are unable to attend on this date, giving reasons. If the reasons are legitimate and you provide the appropriate evidence this will prevent the next letter in sequence from being sent.

2. *Failing to deliver up books and records of a business*

    Bob was trading the business Bob's fisheries. Despite requests from the Official Receiver's office to deliver up the books and records of the business, Bob has failed to deliver up these records. Again requests will be made on the 'three strikes and you're out' basis. Following Bob's failure to respond to all requests, the Official Receiver will arrange a court hearing for the suspension of Bob's discharge.

3. *Failing to provide information regarding income and expenditure*

>As explained in chapter 6, depending on the level of Bob's monthly income and expenditure, he may be asked to sign an IPA agreeing to make monthly payments for the benefit of the bankruptcy estate. If Bob refuses to provide evidence to support his income or expenditure or simply ignored the requests to provide the information this may result in an application for the suspension of Bob's discharge. Alternatively, providing the information but failing to sign an income payments agreement could result in an application for an income payments order (IPO). This is an order by the court enforcing payments from income by the bankrupt.

Bankruptcy Restrictions Orders (BROs)

Prior to the Enterprise Act 2002 all bankrupts were discharged on the third anniversary of their bankruptcy. The Act sought to distinguish between the sheep (who had done no wrong) and the goats (bankrupts that had been dishonest, irresponsible or reckless). The sheep would be discharged sooner and as a counter-balance the Official Receiver may seek to have restrictions imposed upon the goats beyond his date of discharge for between 2 and 15 years. The new legislation came into force on 1 April 2004 and any misconduct before that date falls outside its scope. Bankruptcy restrictions are primarily for protecting the public.

What is a BRO?

Again, as previously explained, bankruptcy usually lasts for exactly one year. During that year the bankrupt is obliged to adhere to certain restrictions and obligations. If a BRO is to be made then the restrictions (not obligations) will be extended beyond the normal year. A BRO will extend the restrictions of bankruptcy for any period between 2 and 15 years depending upon the level of misconduct found.

To Clarify:
The main restrictions of bankruptcy are:

> ➤ You must not obtain credit of £500 or more, either alone or with another person from anyone without first informing that person that you are bankrupt.

> ➤ You must not carry on business (directly or indirectly) in a different name from that in which you were made bankrupt without telling all those with whom you do business the name in which you were made bankrupt.

> ➤ You must not be concerned (directly or indirectly) in promoting, forming or managing a company, or act as a company director (whether or not you are formally appointed as a director), without the court's permission.

> ➤ You may not hold certain public offices.

> ➤ You may not hold office as a Trustee of a charity or a pension fund.

These restrictions will still apply to Bob whilst subject to a BRO for the period ordered by the court.

The main obligations of bankruptcy are:
You must tell your Trustee within 21 days about any property that becomes yours and any increases in your income during your bankruptcy.

The obligations will only apply whilst Bob is an undischarged bankrupt. After 12 months from the bankruptcy order Bob will be discharged from bankruptcy. If a BRO has been ordered he will still receive his discharge from bankruptcy. Once discharged, Bob is no longer bankrupt. The BRO simply means that despite no longer being bankrupt the restrictions of bankruptcy will still apply for the period ordered by the court.

Why have a BRO?

The purpose of a BRO is to protect the public interest. That is, a Bankruptcy Restrictions Order should provide an extended period of protection to the marketplace and creditors in respect of the future conduct of the bankrupt. It should also act as a deterrent to others from acting in a similar manner. In short, if it is proved that a bankrupt has been irresponsible or reckless then there will be repercussions.

How does the Official Receiver evidence a BRO?

Misconduct resulting in a BRO is usually found through the following;

a) Looking into the answers given in the questionnaire (form PIQB) if made bankrupt through a creditors petition, or looking through the answers given on the statement of affairs if made bankrupt through a debtors petition (Bob petitioning for his own bankruptcy). – To get a better understanding of what will be looked at in each question a full analysis has been provided in chapter 8.

b) Bob's answers to questions when interviewed by an Insolvency Examiner. Again the interview revolves around the completed questionnaire (form PIQB) or the completed statement of affairs.

c) Checking through books and records delivered up, be it either business records or personal credit card statements and bank statements.

d) Checking through credit card statements/bank statements requested directly from the credit card companies/banks. Regardless of whether the bankrupt delivers up records, if further investigation is required following an interview the Official Receiver may request copy statements from the companies directly.

e) Whistleblowers: A creditor may call the Official Receiver's office with information regarding possible misconduct by the bankrupt.

What misconduct justifies a BRO?

Whilst the law provides specific matters which amount to misconduct (schedule 4A to The Insolvency Act), the list is not exhaustive. Detailed below are common examples of misconduct found in bankruptcy cases, which result in BROs.

Preference

It is a common misconception with bankrupts that if they borrowed money from somebody, such as a friend or a family member and paid them back in full then that is perfectly acceptable. Depending on circumstances this can be considered as misconduct by the Official Receiver and could result in a BRO.

If it is proved that the bankrupt was insolvent at the time that he repaid the friend/family member, then the payment to this person will be considered as a 'preference' payment as this person was paid in preference over other creditors that have remained outstanding. In other words, the misconduct is that the bankrupt has sought to improve the financial position of his friend/family member whilst other creditors suffer through non payment.

Example – preference:

Last year Bob borrowed £15,000 from Bess (Bob's Extremely Supportive Spouse) for Bob's fisheries to take advantage of a particularly good deal on halibut. Unfortunately, the customers went for cod and his business started to sink. Bob managed to sell the lease to the shop and paid Bess back in full six months later, but he has not made payments to any other creditors. Unfortunately Bob's business loan and main fish suppliers had not been paid for months at the time when he paid Bess back in full.

Clearly Bob's wife was more important to him than his general business creditor, but in financial terms it was wrong to make sure she was paid outright when others received nothing. This transaction is accordingly considered as misconduct by the Official Receiver.

Undervalue transaction

An undervalue transaction is treated in much the same way as a preference payment. If the bankrupt sold an asset (generally to a friend or family member) at an amount less than the asset is worth then this will be considered as misconduct as the asset could have been sold for more. The reason this is considered as misconduct is that the 'undervalue transaction' could have been used to pay off debts to creditors.

Example – Undervalue transaction 1:

Bob jointly owned the matrimonial home with Bess with £50,000 equity. Bob put the house in Bess's sole name, an undervalue transaction of £25,000. Bob was insolvent at the time he made the gift.

Note: The Trustee in bankruptcy would also write to Bob's wife requesting that she repay the £25,000 undervalue transaction to the bankruptcy estate.

Example – Undervalue transaction 2:

Bob was the sole trader of a large parcel delivery business which he had bought some years earlier with a large bank loan. He also had arrears of tax and whilst the business was valued at £200,000, Bob sold the business to his sister for £10,000 - an undervalue transaction of £190,000. Bob was insolvent at the time he made this sale as he owed large sums of money to business creditors.

This will result in a BRO application as if Bob sold the business elsewhere it is likely he would have received £200,000 from the sale and his creditors have lost the additional £190,000 that could have been obtained from the sale and used to pay creditors' debts.

The effect of the transaction makes a difference as to how serious the misconduct is considered to be and the period of restriction sought. Therefore whilst Example 1 and Example 2 are for the same misconduct, the court would order a lesser period of restriction if Bob's wife or sister reimbursed the Trustee.

Trading to the detriment of the crown

There is an old proverb that the only two things you can't avoid in life are death and taxes.

Once Bob's in business he has to tell HM Revenue & Customs (HMRC) how much he owes and send in the forms and payment. If Bob takes advantage of this situation when times get tough, HMRC may not find out until too late and our taxes go up to fund the shortfall. It can therefore be considered misconduct if a bankrupt has neglected to pay crown debts (debts to HM Revenue & Customs for outstanding PAYE/NI/VAT/other taxes). An example is given below:

Example – trading to the detriment of the crown:

Bob was trading a car sales business. Bob owed crown debts for outstanding VAT of £50,000. Bob also owed money to other trade creditors for the purchase of vehicles. These trade creditors had refused to make any further sales to Bob unless he paid them the money they were already owed. In order to continue trading Bob neglected paying his taxes and used this money to pay off his trade creditors in full. When Bob was made bankrupt the VAT debt accounted for the large majority of his total debts. The Official Receiver applied to the court for a BRO as Bob had been neglecting to pay crown monies in order to continue trading his business.

Gambling

Although it is not illegal to gamble, it can be considered an offence when considering a BRO. This is due to the fact that if a bankrupt gambled and lost money, this money could have been used to pay off creditors. The bankrupt effectively gambled with other people's money.

Example – Gambling:

Bob had an internet gambling account. Bob made losses of £20,000 in the last two years. The total amount of money Bob owes to creditors in his bankruptcy totals £25,000. This will be considered by the Official Receiver as misconduct as Bob's gambling losses account for the large proportion of his debts. If Bob had not gambled he would have been able to pay off the vast majority of his creditors. In this instance the Official Receiver would apply to the court for a BRO.

If the Official Receiver seeks a BRO on the grounds of gambling, the Official Receiver will be required to provide sufficient evidence of the gambling. Internet gambling accounts are easily proved as the Official Receiver can obtain an account from the betting company. However, if for example Bob had gambled £20,000 on fruit machines, this would be more difficult to prove. The Official Receiver would rely on cash withdrawals from bank/credit card statements, or if Bob gambled regularly at one place, the Official Receiver may seek identification from staff. The Official Receiver would have to prove that Bob was insolvent at the time he was gambling.

Extravagance / No realistic expectation of repaying debts

If a large proportion of a bankrupt's deficiency (total creditors less any assets) can be attributed to extravagant expenditure, this may result in a BRO.

Example – Extravagance:

Whilst insolvent, Bob purchased two cruise holidays. These holidays cost £10,000 each. Bob also used his credit cards to eat out at restaurants most evenings. Bob had store cards which he regularly used to purchase expensive clothing.

The total of the above expenditure amounts to £27,000. Bob's total deficiency totals £33,000. Therefore Bob's extravagant expenditure amounts to 81% of the deficiency. The above will be considered as misconduct by the Official Receiver and he would seek a BRO from the court, as Bob had been living an extravagant lifestyle at the expense of his creditors.

If the Official Receiver could prove that Bob had been continuing to obtain further credit whilst he was aware or should have been aware of his insolvency, but the spend was not 'extravagant'. A BRO may be sought (for a shorter period than that sought for 'extravagance') due to Bob having no realistic expectation of being able to repay his debts.

Failing to deliver up books and records

Anyone that trades has to keep books and records for tax purposes. Should they go bankrupt these will be required by the Official Receiver; If they are not available the Official Receiver would only say this was misconduct if there was a practical consequence e.g. his investigations into what became of substantial cash withdrawals are hampered due to not being able to check the books and records of Bob's business.

Bankruptcy Restriction Undertakings (BRUs)

If the Official Receiver intends to apply to the court for a BRO then he will first send a copy of his report to the bankrupt informing the bankrupt of his intentions to seek a BRO. The bankrupt has the opportunity to defend the BRO at court or to undertake. The Official Receiver will inform the bankrupt of the period of restriction he will be seeking from the court.

A Bankruptcy Restrictions Undertaking (BRU) is an agreement whereby Bob accepts the misconduct stated in the Official Receiver's report and agrees to abide by the restriction rather than go to court. The Official Receiver will offer an undertaking at a lower period than the period the Official Receiver would seek from the court, to reflect both Bob's acceptance of the misconduct and the cost savings to the state by avoiding a trial. The discount given on an undertaking is generally one year.

Example – BRU:

Bob has received documentation from the Official Receiver regarding a report to the court seeking a bankruptcy restrictions order for an alleged preference payment made to his brother which has not been repaid. The letter from the Official Receiver states that the Official Receiver will seek a period of restriction of 6 years. However, Bob may sign an undertaking for a period of 5 years.

Bob agrees the report is factually correct and decides to take the offer of a BRU. The BRU will then be signed on behalf of the Secretary of State and filed at court. Having agreed to the undertaking Bob has now had the restrictions (not obligations) of his bankruptcy extended by 5 years.

Bob could have filed his defence and attended the court for the hearing of a BRO, with the intention of getting the period shortened. However, it is worth bearing in mind that if sufficient evidence is not provided in defence, there is always the chance that the court will order a period beyond that of which the Official Receiver is seeking.

It is advantageous to the Official Receiver to obtain a BRU as although the bankrupt's restrictions would likely be for a shorter period than that of a BRO, it avoids a court hearing. The Official Receiver or his Assistant (depending on who attends the hearing) will very likely have to spend many hours, perhaps days, preparing for the court hearing and the judge that takes the hearing will likely spend time reading the papers. Then there is the time taken for the actual trial. Obviously this time and cost is saved if Bob agrees to an undertaking and it is fair to reward Bob with a reduction in the tariff of his undertaking.

Negotiating a BRU

If Bob received a letter from the Official Receiver stating the Official Receiver's intention to seek an order from the court for a BRO, it may be possible for the bankrupt to negotiate an undertaking with the Official Receiver. In the above example, the Official Receiver was seeking an order of 6 years and offering an undertaking of 5 years to Bob. Bob may call the Official Receiver stating that although he agrees to the misconduct alleged he does not agree that the period sought is fair.

In order to negotiate the period down, it would not be acceptable for Bob to just say that the period sought is unfair. He will need to provide some defence to part of the allegation made, or provide some mitigating circumstances. In this particular case Bob may have persuaded his brother to make full or partial repayment of the preference. This would warrant a reduction in the period.

Prosecutions

If any criminal matters come to light when investigating the bankrupt's financial affairs then this can result in the Official Receiver submitting a statement of facts to Business Enterprise and Regulatory Reform (BERR) solicitors, which can then result in a criminal prosecution.

Following are a series of common areas of misconduct found in bankruptcy cases, resulting in prosecution. It is worth noting that most criminal offences will also result in a bankruptcy restrictions order (BRO).

Fraud

If a bankrupt has lied in an application in order to obtain credit then this is a criminal offence. If this is proved a statement of facts will be submitted outlining the criminal matter.

Example – Fraud:

Bob attended the Official Receiver's office for interview. At the interview he stated that he had been unemployed for the last five years. The Examiner appointed in Bob's case decided it was necessary to obtain copies of loan applications for the loans that Bob had obtained during the period of his unemployment, as loan applications usually ask the applicant to state their salary. When the Examiner received the applications it was evident that Bob had been dishonest in three of his loan applications, stating that he was earning an annual salary of £25,000.

Bob was invited back to the Official Receiver's office for a second interview. In this interview the Examiner relayed Bob's comments from the first interview, stating that he had been unemployed for five years and showed Bob copies of the loan applications. Bob was then given the opportunity to explain his actions.

Bob admitted to having falsely obtained credit stating that he was desperate for the money and knew he had to lie in the applications in order to obtain the credit. Bob stated that he did have every intention to repay the debt.

Due to the above, the Official Receiver submitted a statement of facts regarding the criminal matter.

Breaching the Bankruptcy Restrictions:

Obtaining Credit

As listed in the restrictions and obligations imposed on a bankrupt. One of the restrictions states:

> ➢ You must not obtain credit of £500 or more, either alone or with another person from anyone without first informing that person that you are bankrupt. You may open a new bank or building society account but you should tell the bank or building society when opening the account (and must tell the bank or building society before incurring an overdraft) that you are bankrupt.

Whilst bankrupt and therefore subject to the above restriction, if a bankrupt were to obtain credit of £500 or more without first informing that person that he was subject to a bankruptcy order this would be a criminal offence.

Example – Obtaining credit:

In this example Bob is a self employed Carpet fitter. Three months into Bob's bankruptcy, he approached Carl's Carpet Market Ltd, a local supplier and Bob purchased £3,000 worth of goods on credit which he didn't settle. The Official Receiver received a letter of complaint from Carl Pile the director of Carl's Carpet Market Ltd. Mr Pile was displeased as he has just become aware that Bob is bankrupt and Bob has been obtaining goods on credit from his company. Mr Pile confirmed to the Official Receiver that he would not have granted the credit to Bob had he known that Bob was subject to a bankruptcy order.

In the circumstances, the Official Receiver submitted a statement of facts regarding the criminal matter.

Acting in the management of a company

As listed in the restrictions and obligations imposed on a bankrupt, one of the restrictions states:

- ➢ You must not be concerned (directly or indirectly) in promoting, forming or managing a company, or act as a company director (whether or not you are formally appointed as a director), without the court's permission.

Example – Acting in the management of a company:

When Bob attended the Official Receiver's office for interview, he did not disclose at interview or in his questionnaire that he was currently a director of Bob's Hobs Ltd, which specialised in the sale and fitting of cookers.

The directorship came to light when a dissatisfied customer contacted the Official Receiver to complain. In the circumstances the Official Receiver submitted a statement of facts regarding the criminal matter.

Failure to deliver up all property to the Trustee in bankruptcy

If a bankrupt did not to the best of his knowledge and belief disclose to the Trustee all property comprised in his estate, this would be a crime.

Example – Failure to deliver up all property to the Trustee in bankruptcy:

When initially interviewed by an Examiner at the Official Receiver's office. Bob failed to disclose a property in his possession. Bob did not disclose the property at interview, or in the bankruptcy questionnaire (Form PIQB).

Some years later, it came to light that Bob owned a property that he had failed to disclose when made bankrupt. Bob was invited back to the Official Receiver's office for a further interview to explain why he had not disclosed the property at this time.

Bob was unable to provide a sufficient explanation and the Official Receiver submitted a statement of facts detailing the prosecutable offence.

Chapter 8

Bankruptcy – Demystifying the investigation

The Official Receiver is an officer of the court and a civil servant within the Department for Business Enterprise and Regulatory Reform (BERR). For most of the UK population their principle experience of bankruptcy is the unpleasant experiences of a host of characters in classical literature and the title investigation probably carries connotations of police and criminality. This is, however, a world apart from modern day insolvency in which a bankruptcy interview is a preliminary investigation which seeks to test the explanation of the cause of insolvency.

In that respect Bob may be able to help us dispel some myths. Let us explore a series of scenarios in which Bob has provided an explanation of why he has failed, compare it to the facts on how debts have arisen and reach a conclusion as to the cause of bankruptcy. To put Bob's interview in context, fewer than 3% of cases involve civil misconduct and fewer still involve criminality; put another way, in 97% of cases the Official Receiver concludes that there is no misconduct or there are insufficient reasons to justify further proceedings.

This chapter is designed as a guide to understanding the consequences of answers given when completing the questionnaire that must be completed when made bankrupt via a creditor's petition, and the statement of affairs that is to be completed and handed in at court in order to petition for your own bankruptcy.

The Statement of affairs and the Questionnaire (Form PIQB) ask essentially the same questions. Therefore I have based this chapter on questions given from the questionnaire and next to each question have stated in brackets ( ) the number of the corresponding/similar question given in the Statement of Affairs (SOA).

To each of the <u>key</u> questions asked in the questionnaire/statement of affairs, there is a series of possible answers given by Bob. Each answer surrounds different circumstances concerning Bob. Likely repercussions to each of the answers to the key questions are given, stating clearly if an answer is likely to result in a criminal prosecution or a BRO.

It is important to complete all sections of the questionnaire/Statement of Affairs as fully as possible. However, in this chapter I am mainly focusing on questions where misconduct can often be found.

Please read through this section carefully.

Bankruptcy Preliminary Information Questionnaire Form PIQB

The step by step guide – as completed by Bob

Section 5 of the Perjury Act 1911

Page 3

At the front of this questionnaire Bob will be asked to read and sign to Section 5 of the Perjury Act 1911.

> # Your personal details

Pages 4 to 6

Bob is required to complete a series of questions detailing personal information such as his full name, date of birth, NI number etc.

Key question:

> 1.12 Are you, or in the last 5 years have you been, involved in proceedings for divorce, separation or the dissolution of a civil partnership? (SOA question 1.12)

Purpose of question:

To ascertain the movement and transfer of assets as a result of the divorce proceedings, and to establish whether any of the assets transferred will form assets within Bob's personal bankruptcy proceedings. If he answers yes to this question he may be asked to provide a copy of the divorce settlement, including details of the solicitors who were acting.

In the majority of cases the Examiner will merely obtain confirmation that the divorce settlement was a formal agreement sealed at the court. However, if it was an informal agreement in which Bob's creditors clearly lost out, for example that Bob's half interest in the marital home was transferred into his wife's sole name, the Official Receiver may seek to recover money for the creditors by asking the court to reverse the transaction and to seek a BRO against the bankrupt.

Possible Answers:

> a) Yes
>
> b) No

Robin Meynell

Possible repercussions to answers:

a) This will produce further questioning at interview. Such as, was there a financial settlement within the divorce proceedings, be it either formal or informal? Bob will in fact be required to disclose such information in the following question, number 1.13.

b) This will not produce further questioning.

Key question:

1.15 Have you been bankrupt before? (SOA question 1.14)

Purpose of question:

To establish if Bob had previously been made bankrupt, and if so, when was he discharged from his previous bankruptcy.

Misconduct can flow from the answer to this question. The Examiner will first check when Bob was discharged from his previous bankruptcy. If Bob was discharged prior to April 2004, any misconduct that may have occurred would not result in a BRO. In this instance the Examiner will not carry out any further investigation. If Bob was discharged from his previous bankruptcy after April 2004, the Examiner may look to see if Bob had defaulted on any of the restrictions or obligations he should have adhered to whilst bankrupt.

For example, in the restrictions and obligations form, you may not obtain credit of £500 or more whilst bankrupt unless you inform that person of your status before the obtaining of such credit.

If Bob had previously been made bankrupt, the Examiner may look into whether any of Bob's current debts were obtained for more than

£500 whilst he was an undischarged bankrupt (during his previous bankruptcy).

It is also possible, if previously made bankrupt, that if Bob had not cooperated fully at the time of his previous bankruptcy that the bankruptcy discharge date had been suspended. In such circumstances (if the suspension had not been lifted) all debts claimed in Bob's current bankruptcy would be for debts obtained whilst an undischarged bankrupt.

Possible Answers:

a) Yes

b) No

Possible repercussions to answers:

a) If for example Bob acquired credit of more than £500 whilst an undischarged bankrupt in his previous bankruptcy, this could result in a BRO and could be a prosecutable offence, depending on the period and level of credit obtained.

b) This will not produce further questioning. However, the Examiner will be required to check the Insolvency Service database to check if Bob has had a previous bankruptcy registered on the system.

Assets

Pages 7 to 10

In this section Bob is asked to disclose all assets (any items he owns worth any significant value).

Key question:

> 2.1 Please list everything you own including assets of your business (if any) and its approximate amount or value. (SOA question 3.1)

Purpose of question:

To identify assets owned by Bob that will form assets within the bankruptcy estate (pot for creditors).

Possible Answers:

The question lists a series of asset types such as Cash in bank, motor vehicles, stock in trade, premium bonds, etc. Bob is required to list under each category whether he owns any such items.

Possible repercussions to answers:

If Bob were to deliberately not disclose an asset in an attempt to hide this asset from the Trustee in bankruptcy, this would be a criminal offence. Depending on the value of the asset this could result in both a bankruptcy restrictions order and prosecution.

Key question:

> 2.3 In the last 5 years have you transferred, sold or given away any of your personal possessions or business assets at less than their value or less than their cost? (SOA question 3.5)

Purpose of question:

The law allows the court to reverse such transactions, if Bob was unable to pay his debts at the time, or became so by giving the assets away.

Possible answers:

a) Yes, I gave my car to my son. The car was worth approximately £15,000 at the time.

b) Yes, I sold my car to my son for £1,000. It was probably worth £15,000 at the time.

c) Yes, I gave my car to my father. I owed him £15,000. The car was worth approximately £15,000 so this was given to him in repayment of the loan.

d) No.

Possible repercussions to answers:

a) Bob gifted a car worth approximately £15,000 to his son. This will be considered as an 'undervalue transaction' worth £15,000. Bob has effectively given away £15,000 that could have been paid towards his creditors. This will be considered as misconduct by the Official Receiver and is likely to result in a BRO. What's more, Bob's son will be requested to repay the £15,000 'undervalue transaction' to the Trustee in bankruptcy.

If Bob's son were to ignore the Trustee's demands for repayment, it is very difficult for the Trustee to enforce the issue and therefore unlikely that he will. However, if Bob's son does repay the debt this will reduce the period of the BRO to be made against Bob.

b) This will be treated in exactly the same way as (a). However rather than the 'undervalue transaction' being £15,000 it is in this example £14,000.

c) Although Bob's father was owed £15,000 and was therefore a creditor of Bob's. The fact that Bob repaid a debt in full to his father will be considered by the Official Receiver/Trustee to be a 'preference payment' to his father. This is because Bob has paid a debt to his father in preference to his other creditors. This is considered as misconduct and is likely to result in a BRO and Bob's father will be requested to repay the £15,000 preference to the Trustee in bankruptcy. Bob feels this is unfair. He has paid his father (a creditor) back money that was owed and does not see why his father should have to repay the sum to the Trustee in bankruptcy. Unfortunately Bob, that's how the system works. If Bob's father does repay the debt, the period of Bob's BRO will be reduced.

d) This will not produce further questioning.

Important Note:

The previous question (2.2) is very similar. This question focuses on assets gifted, sold, or transferred after the date of the bankruptcy order. The purpose of this question is to identify any assets owned at the date of the bankruptcy order and what became of them. Any asset owned at the date of the bankruptcy order becomes an asset of the bankruptcy estate. Bob does not have the right to sell assets which fall into the bankruptcy and to do so would be misconduct.

Key question:

2.4 In the last 2 years have you made any payment to a creditor, other than in the ordinary course of business, with a view to improving the position of that creditor in case you became subject to insolvency/bankruptcy proceedings? (SOA question 3.6)

Purpose of question:

This question is designed to find out whether the bankrupt has preferentially paid one creditor over his other creditors. Possible answers and repercussions to such answers can be closely related to the previous question.

Possible answers:

- a) Yes, I paid £14,000 to my Uncle.

- b) Yes, I paid £15,000 to the Inland Revenue.

- c) No

Possible repercussions to answers:

- a) Bob paid £14,000 to his Uncle with the intention of improving the position of his Uncle's finances before he went bankrupt. In this example Bob has preferentially paid his Uncle over his other creditors. This preference payment would be treated similarly to the preference example given in chapter 7 and is likely to result in a BRO.

- b) Although Bob preferentially paid £15,000 to the Inland Revenue, this is very unlikely to be considered as misconduct and no further action is likely to be taken. As explained in chapter 7 preference payments considered are almost always payments made to family or friends.

- c) No further action will be taken.

Motor Vehicles

Page 13

In this section Bob is required to list details of all motor vehicles he currently owns or has disposed of in the last 12 months.

Robin Meynell

Key question:

5.1 *Do you own a motor vehicle or have you disposed of any motor vehicle in the 12 months before the bankruptcy petition was presented? (SOA question 3.7)*

5.2 *If yes, give details*

Purpose of question:

The main purpose of this question is to receive information of possible assets owned by Bob, be it a motor vehicle or cash received from the sale of a motor vehicle. Also, to establish if any assets have been sold at an undervalue.

Possible answers:

a) Bob owns a Ford Escort worth £500

b) Bob owns an Alfa Romeo Spider worth £5,000

c) Bob owns a vehicle subject to a hire purchase agreement worth £5,000 and subject to finance of £6,000

d) Bob sold his Alfa Romeo Spider worth £5,000 six months ago

e) Bob sold his vehicle subject to a hire purchase agreement four months ago

Possible repercussions to answers:

a) The car will be exempt from the bankruptcy proceedings if it falls under the provisions of Section 283(2) of the Insolvency Act 1986 (as explained in chapter 6), if Bob requires this vehicle for work purposes. If the vehicle is not exempt, it will be realised (sold) for the benefit of the bankruptcy estate (pot of money held for creditors).

b) If the vehicle falls within the exemption as per Section 283(2), then due to the fact that the vehicle is worth more than the accepted capped value of £2,000 the vehicle will have to be sold. £2,000 from the sale of the vehicle will be returned to Bob to purchase a vehicle that is considered to be an acceptable value. The remaining £3,000 received from the sale of the vehicle will be put into the bankruptcy estate for the benefit of Bob's creditors. If Bob's vehicle does not fall under the exemptions stated in Section 283(2), Bob's Alfa Romeo Spider will be sold and the full £5,000 proceeds received from the sale will be put into the bankruptcy estate.

c) The Hire Purchase (HP) company will be notified of the bankruptcy order by the Trustee in bankruptcy. As explained in chapter 6, it is likely that the HP company will agree to continue the agreement with the bankrupt rather than repossess the vehicle and make a loss.

d) Bob will be asked to explain the whereabouts of the £5,000 received from the sale of the car. If this money was spent, Bob will be required to explain this expenditure. Bob may also be asked how much he believed the car was worth when it was sold. This is to establish if the vehicle was sold at an undervalue. As explained earlier, an undervalue transaction may result in a BRO.

e) The purpose of a Hire Purchase (HP) agreement is that the vehicle belongs to the HP company until the debt to them has been paid in full. Bob therefore does not own the vehicle and may not legally sell the vehicle. This could possibly result in Bob being prosecuted and may also result in a BRO.

Properties (including land)

Pages 15 to 17

In this section Bob is required to list all properties that he has resided at or otherwise has had an interest in within the last five years.

Key question:

7.1 List **all** properties that you currently own, rent, lease or otherwise have an interest in **and also** any properties that you have owned, rented, or otherwise had an interest in during the past 5 years. Include everywhere that you have lived in the last 5 years and any premises you are currently using, or have previously used, for business purposes. (SOA questions 8.1 through to 9.1)

Purpose of question:

The main purpose to this question is to make sure that no assets have been missed that could benefit the bankruptcy estate. Also, as previously explained all bankruptcies are advertised in the London Gazette and a local newspaper. It may be necessary to update the advertisement if it does not state Bob's previous address.

Possible answers and repercussions:

When Bob lists the properties, if for example he fails to list his property in Spain worth £70,000 in this section, or on any other section of the questionnaire, or at interview, this is a serious offence. The deliberate non-disclosure of an asset (particularly of such significant value), will very likely result in Bob being prosecuted and a BRO.

Endowment, other life policies and other insurance policies

Page 18

The purpose of this section is again to establish whether there are assets to be realised for the benefit of the bankruptcy estate.

Key question:

> 8.1 Do you have or have you had any endowment or other life policies? (SOA question 3.2)

Purpose of question:

To obtain information regarding assets that may be realisable for the purposes of the bankruptcy estate.

Possible answers:

> a) Bob owns a life insurance policy
>
> b) Bob owns an endowment policy worth £10,000
>
> c) Bob jointly owns an endowment policy worth £10,000

Possible repercussions to answers:

> a) The life insurance policy will form an asset within the bankruptcy proceedings even if it does not presently have a surrender value. Whilst Bob could cancel the policy and take another, Bob's health may have deteriorated since taking the policy and he may want to continue paying into this life insurance policy as the premiums on a new one would be more expensive. If so he would have to buy it back from the bankruptcy for a fixed fee

of £50. If Bob concealed a policy that had value it would likely lead to a BRO or prosecution. However, if he concealed one without value and continued paying the premiums without buying the policy back and subsequently died, the payout would go to the bankruptcy and not his loved ones.

> There is nothing to stop you from closing a life policy and opening a new policy after the date of the bankruptcy order. The advantage of this is that you would not then have to pay the £50 fee to the Trustee.

b) This will form an asset within the bankruptcy proceedings and will be realised for the benefit of the bankruptcy estate.

c) Bob's interest in this policy will form an asset within the bankruptcy proceedings. This policy is jointly owned with Bob's wife and the Trustee in bankruptcy will surrender £5,000 being 50% of the balance in the endowment policy.

Items you have but do not own

Page 19

The purpose of this section is to ensure that any asset in the bankrupt's possession that he/she does not believe to be belonging to himself/herself is declared in the bankruptcy proceedings. The Trustee in bankruptcy can then determine whether the asset is in fact belonging to the bankrupt and whether it does or does not form an asset within the bankruptcy proceedings.

Key question:

> 10.1 Do you have in your possession or control anything (including goods, equipment, and vehicles) that does not belong to you? (SOA question 3.9)

Purpose of question:

To identify other peoples assets to make sure they are not sold by mistake, or costs wasted insuring or protecting them.

Possible answers:

a) No

b) Yes, I drive my wife's vehicle.

Possible repercussions to answers:

a) No further action will be taken.

b) If Bob is stating that the vehicle is his wife's car because it is registered in her name, this does not necessarily mean that the vehicle belongs to his wife. If Bob purchased the vehicle and is the main user of the vehicle the Trustee may determine that the vehicle in fact belongs to Bob. Other matters to take into consideration are who pays the insurance on the vehicle and who pays for the maintenance on the vehicle. Again, if this is Bob then this would strengthen the belief that the vehicle, although registered in his wife's name, is really Bob's vehicle and therefore unless exempt, will form an asset within the bankruptcy. If the Trustee agrees that the vehicle does belong to Bob's wife then of course this will not form an asset within the bankruptcy.

Robin Meynell

> # Hire Purchase and finance agreements

Page 20

The purpose of this section is to establish what assets in the bankrupt's possession are subject to hire purchase or finance agreements. If the bankrupt does owe money to a hire purchase company then it is important for the Trustee to establish the whereabouts of the asset.

Key question:

> 12.1 Do you owe any money to a finance company for items on hire purchase, lease or conditional sale? (SOA question 3.1+3.7)

Purpose of question:

If an asset is subject to finance, the company will need to be informed of the bankruptcy and they will need to show that the nature of the agreement means that they own the asset. If they can't show that they own the asset it can be sold and used to pay creditors.

Possible answers:

> a) Yes
>
> b) Yes (alternative reason)
>
> c) No

Possible repercussions to answers:

> a) Bob acquired a Fiat Punto on a hire purchase (HP) agreement in March 2005. The vehicle is kept on Bob's driveway. It is estimated to be worth £3,000 and is subject to finance of £4,000. The Trustee in bankruptcy will need to notify the

HP company of Bob's bankruptcy. The HP company may then repossess the vehicle. However it is likely that they will allow Bob to keep the car and continue to pay his monthly instalments, as this may be their best chance of being repaid.

b) Bob acquired a Fiat Punto on a hire purchase (HP) agreement in March 2005. Bob sold this vehicle in December 2005 for £5,000. Bob still owes £5,000 to Crazy Auto Finance Ltd. Bob has sold an asset that does not belong to him. Bob retained the proceeds from the sale and did not pay off his debt to the finance company. This is a criminal matter and may result in both a BRO and prosecution.

c) Bob does not owe money to any finance companies for items on hire purchase, lease or conditional sale. No further action would be taken on this matter by the Examiner.

List of creditors

Page 22

In this section the bankrupt is required to complete a table listing all creditors, with addresses, the amount owing to each creditor, the date each debt was originally incurred, and a brief description as to what each debt was for. As these details are used to send information to creditors, if the bankrupt lists full details for every creditor it is more likely that the creditor will update their records and stop sending threatening letters to the bankrupt. (SOA Section 4)

Table of creditors to complete

Name of Creditor	Address	Amount Owing £	Date incurred	What was the debt for?

It is worth noting that any misconduct found by the Examiner must post date April 2004 to qualify for a bankruptcy restrictions order. Therefore any debts incurred prior to April 2004 are not likely to be investigated as rigorously.

Credit card statements are likely to be reviewed/investigated by the Examiner following the interview. The bankrupt will be expected to deliver up all credit card statements at the interview. If statements are not delivered, the Examiner is likely to request copies directly from the credit card companies.

If the bankrupt obtained a consolidation loan, this is likely to have paid off several debts including credit cards. As those credit card companies are no longer creditors (having been paid off by the consolidation loan) it is unlikely that the bankrupt will be requested to deliver statements to the Official Receiver's office for these cards.

Present income + Outgoings

Pages 25 to 27 of questionnaire (SOA Sections 6 and 7)

When completing details concerning income and expenditure it is important to understand that this information will be used to calculate whether an income payments agreement (IPA) can be set up. If you are to complete a questionnaire/Statement of Affairs, before completing this section, I suggest you read back through the explanation and examples given through Bob's different financial circumstances in chapter 6.

Betting and Gambling

Page 28

Key question:

> 19.1 Have you lost any money by betting, gambling or similar activities in the last 2 years? (SOA question 11.3)
>
> 19.2 If **Yes**, how much do you think you have lost? (SOA question 11.3)

Purpose of question

As explained in Chapter 7, gambling can result in a bankruptcy restrictions order due to the fact that the bankrupt had been reckless/irresponsible with his creditors' money. In other words, the money that the bankrupt lost on gambling could have been used to pay off a proportion/all of his debts.

Directorships

Page 28

Key question:

> 20.1 Are you, or in the last 5 years have you been, a director or involved in the management of a company? (SOA question 1.17)
>
> 20.2 If **Yes**, give details (SOA question 1.17)

Robin Meynell

Purpose of question

To establish the legal nature of any trade carried out and whether the bankrupt is currently a director of a limited company.

Possible repercussions to answers:

With few exceptions, any debts incurred by the company cannot be claimed in the bankruptcy. The principle exceptions are where the director signed a personal guarantee or reused the name of an insolvent company without ensuring that the appropriate exceptions applied. The reuse of an insolvent company's name is also a criminal offence as is acting as a director whilst bankrupt without the permission of the court.

Having read through this chapter

You should now have a much better understanding of the purpose to each of the key questions asked. The Statement of Affairs and the Questionnaire (Form PIQB) ask essentially the same questions; The technical difference is that the Statement of Affairs is a sworn document whereas the PIQB answers are subject to the Perjury Act – in practice both have the same impact and whilst admitting misconduct in either could be used in evidence for civil proceedings such as BROs, under the law, a lie in these documents may also be used against you in criminal proceedings.

Therefore, it is essential you answer all questions as accurately as possible.

Chapter 9

Annulment (Cancellation) of bankruptcy

Once a bankruptcy order is made Bob cannot get rid of it merely by changing his mind if he had presented his own petition or, on paying the petition debt, if someone else had made him bankrupt. If Bob 'wanted out', he would have to get the bankruptcy formally cancelled. The cancellation of a bankruptcy order is known as an annulment and once an annulment is obtained then it is as if the bankruptcy order had never been made.

There are four main grounds on which Bob can apply for an annulment:

1. If the bankruptcy order 'ought not to have been made'.

2. If all bankruptcy debts are either paid in full or are secured to the satisfaction of the court.

3. Creditors have approved an Individual Voluntary Arrangement.

4. Creditors have approved a Fast Track Voluntary Arrangement

However, the most appropriate approach to an application will often turn on the practicalities such as the likely costs and whether Bob is trading.

Once made bankrupt, were Bob solvent (i.e. his assets exceed his debts), he should contact the Official Receiver immediately if he intends to apply for an annulment to discuss his options and the practical consequences.

If an Insolvency Practitioner (IP) is appointed, the fees will eat into Bob's assets. In many circumstances the appointment of an IP is unavoidable, but if he were in a position to pay all of his debts he may be much better off applying for an annulment himself, with or without the assistance of a solicitor and ask that the Official Receiver refrain from having an IP appointed as his Trustee.

All bankruptcies are advertised in both a local newspaper and in the London Gazette. If Bob does not want the order advertised he will need to ask the court for a stay of advertisement. Bob will ask the court by way of a written "application" and the decision will be made at a "hearing". If he informs the Official Receiver immediately that he is applying for a stay of advertisement it is likely that the Official Receiver will ensure that the advertisement is not published in the time between his application and it being heard by the court.

Stopping the advert does not stop the proceedings and Bob may also wish to apply to the court for a stay of proceedings. If the proceedings are stayed then it may prevent most of the Official Receiver's costs and the requirements for him to attend the Official Receiver's office for interview and to complete the questionnaire (Form PIQB).

How to put forward your application to annul the bankruptcy

It is possible for Bob to do this himself if he does not wish to incur further costs such as solicitor's fees. However if at all unsure, it may be advisable to seek assistance from a solicitor who has experience in dealing with bankruptcy annulment applications. The following scenarios illustrate the differing approaches to an application for annulment, dependent upon the grounds being put to the court.

1. If applying for an annulment on the grounds that the order ought not to have been made

As soon as Bob had decided to go for an annulment he contacted the Official Receiver's office. Bob said he had reached an agreement with the petitioner before the hearing to pay the debt in three instalments over the next three months and that he in turn had been told they would not seek bankruptcy at the hearing. He informed the Examiner of his intentions to apply for an annulment and to also apply to the court in the first instance for a stay of proceedings and stay of advertisement. Bob then contacted the court to put forward the applications for stays.

Bob printed the form titled 'Ordinary Application' from The Insolvency Service website at www.insolvency.gov.uk. To do this he logged onto the site and clicked on 'forms', then 'forms for England and Wales'. Having scrolled down the various forms available for downloading, Bob found and printed off the form titled 'Ordinary Application'. Bob could have alternatively requested a copy of the application form from his local court. Bob wrote the above ground on the form. With this application, Bob attached a statement explaining the reasons as to why he believed the bankruptcy order should not have been made. Bob made this statement by affidavit, which is a sworn document before a solicitor or an officer of the court. As the Official Receiver is an officer of the court, Bob decided to get his statement sworn at the Official Receiver's office as the Official Receiver does not charge a fee for this service.

Bob now wanted to get rid of the bankruptcy as soon as possible and pushed for a hearing that week and in the circumstances the court was able to fit him in. Once Bob received a hearing date for the application he informed all parties concerned with details of the hearing. These were:

- The Official Receiver, and

- The Petitioner (the creditor that petitioned for Bob's bankruptcy)

- If an IP was appointed rather than The Official Receiver as Trustee, Bob would need to have informed the IP as well.

2. If applying for an annulment on the grounds that all bankruptcy debts have been paid in full or secured to the satisfaction of the court.

As soon as Bob had decided to go for an annulment he contacted the Official Receiver's office to inform the Examiner of his intentions to apply for an annulment. However, on this ground, the law says that it takes at least 28 days for the hearing to be heard. As Bob was trading, this threw up a problem, as under the law the Official Receiver does not have the power to trade. To overcome this, Bob could:

- make a separate application to give the Official Receiver the power;

- get an IP appointed as Trustee who was allowed to trade,

- shut up shop pending the hearing or

- ask the court to suspend the bankruptcy (stay it) until it heard his annulment application.

As to costs, the Official Receiver would charge a fixed fee of £1,715 for the administration, but he would charge more if he had to deal with Bob's assets and pay creditors. Whilst this was less than an IP would charge, Bob wanted to avoid this if possible and he could avoid these additional costs altogether if his wife paid creditors directly using her savings. Another option was to get the court to order a different payment method, such as allowing his solicitor to receive the sale proceeds of his house and to pay creditors direct from their "client account". With such options Bob must balance the likely saving (reduced fees) against the additional legal costs.

Bob knew an IP would charge costs to trade and decided to apply to the court in the first instance for a stay of proceedings and stay of advertisement and contacted the court to put forward the application for stays.

After Bob had informed the Official Receiver's office of his intention to apply for an annulment, he was sent a Statement of Affairs to complete. This is different to the Statement of Affairs that would be completed by a person petitioning for their own bankruptcy.

In this statement of affairs Bob was required to list all creditors that he had at the time the bankruptcy order was made together with a list of his assets. The Official Receiver then contacted the creditors to check how much they were owed.

In the meantime Bob's wife Bess paid off all of his debts and sent the Official Receiver copies of receipts from each creditor confirming that their debt had been paid in full. Bob also had a mortgage on his and Bess's home. He did not have to pay this off as the mortgagee confirmed that they would rely on their security and did not need to be paid through the bankruptcy. On receipt of the confirmations from creditors the Official Receiver was satisfied that all debts had been paid and sent a report to the court confirming that to the best of his knowledge all of Bob's debts had been paid or secured.

It is important to note that when applying for an annulment on this ground it is not just the petitioning creditor that needs to be paid, it is all of Bob's unsecured creditors the bankruptcy costs and his solicitor's costs. In this scenario Bob had to pay the petitioning creditor's fees along with the Official Receiver's fixed fees for administering the bankruptcy of £1,715. If an IP had been appointed as Trustee, Bob would have also have had to pay the IP's fees.

3. If applying following the approval of an Individual Voluntary Arrangement (IVA)

Another alternative for Bob to obtain an annulment from bankruptcy is to then seek an IVA, as outlined in chapter 1. This can be a very practical option were Bob solvent but his assets illiquid - namely his assets were well in excess of his liabilities, but his circumstances were such that he had no one to turn to pay his debts off and his assets were such that they could not be quickly turned into cash.

Once an IVA has been approved there is a 28 day appeal window in which a creditor can change their mind and ask the court to overturn the arrangement. Once that period has passed Bob can ask the court to annul the bankruptcy order which is largely dealt with as a formality.

4. If applying on the approval of a Fast Track Voluntary Arrangement (FTVA)

If Bob's circumstances fit the requirements of a Fast-track Voluntary Arrangement (FTVA) then this may be a good option to take in order to get his bankruptcy annulled. The process is only available to bankrupts and is a streamlined version of an IVA. An FTVA is cheaper as it does not have all the checks, balances and costs necessary in a trading IVA and it is accordingly only appropriate for non-trading simple proposals. To illustrate, following bankruptcy Bob attended the Official Receiver's office for interview and as Bob's Creditors were small and he had minimal assets, an FTVA was an option as a way out of his bankruptcy.

The purpose of an FTVA is to offer creditors more than they are likely to receive from the bankruptcy. Bob considered his main options were to:

- Offer a monthly payment for a longer period than that of an Income Payments Agreement (IPA) in bankruptcy. As the Official Receiver obtains an IPA for 3 years, Bob considered offering the same monthly payment for up to a further 2 years giving a total period of 5 years.

- Offer a lump sum payment from a third party such as a family member or a friend.

It was Bob's responsibility to put forward the proposal to the Official Receiver who would then review Bob's proposal and decide whether he felt it would be likely that creditors would accept it.

Bob's total creditors amounted to £12,000, he had no assets, but was able to offer a payment of £150 each month from his surplus income for 42 months (3½ years) and Bess (Bob's Extremely Supportive Spouse) would contribute a lump sum payment of £5,000.

After reviewing the proposal the Official Receiver agreed to act as Nominee and put Bob's proposal forward to his creditors. As explained in Chapter 1, for an IVA, a creditors meeting will be arranged to consider the proposal. At the meeting, creditors may request various changes to the proposal before accepting it. The approach is different for an FTVA. The proposal for an FTVA is sent to creditors - there is no meeting. Creditors can choose to vote in favour of the proposal or vote against the proposal. There is no provision for the proposal to be altered. Furthermore, only the Official Receiver can act as Nominee and Supervisor in an FTVA, and creditors can not nominate an Insolvency Practitioner in his place.

Of the creditors that choose to vote, if there is a 75% vote (in terms of the amount of monies owed) in favour of the proposal then it will be approved and the Official Receiver will become the Supervisor of the FTVA. Creditors that choose not to vote, but are in receipt of the notice of the proposal will be legally bound by the FTVA if it is approved. Fortunately over 75% of the value of the voting creditors regarding Bob's proposal were in favour of the FTVA proposal which was therefore approved.

Bob had to find the following up front fees:

- £35 for registering the FTVA with the Secretary of State

- £300 fixed fee for the Official Receiver's fee as 'Nominee'

Once the proposal was accepted there were additional fees, but these were paid from the lump sum and monthly contributions:

- 15% of the £11,300 raised for the FTVA to cover the Official Receiver's fee as Supervisor.

- A fixed fee of £857.50 for the Official Receiver administering the bankruptcy, which is half the usual fee

- As Bob was made bankrupt by a creditor, they are repaid their petition costs.

Chapter 10

How to manage debt

Having read the first 9 chapters of this book you will now have a thorough understanding of the various different options available to remedy debt. Bob has provided you with a valuable insight into Individual Voluntary Arrangement's (IVAs), Debt Relief Order's (DROs), Debt Management Plans (DMPs) and in great detail, the various processes involved in bankruptcy.

If you have opted for one of the above remedies, you will now be free (or virtually free) of debt!

If so, it is now (I am sure you will agree) vitally important that you remain debt free. This chapter is not intended to patronise the reader. There are various books available on managing debts. These books tend to be full of useless information. A few good points are stretched, and gaps are filled with long drawn out points thrown in to pad out the book. These points are often very patronising. This is because remaining debt free is largely down to common sense. Most people could put together a list of ideas on how to better look after their finances. Putting these ideas into practice however is not so easy.

Therefore, in order not to condescend, following are straight to the point suggestions of what I believe to be the best methods in keeping your finances under control.

Income against expenditure

In Chapter 6, I explained the 'Income Payment Agreement' (IPA). The IPA is a method in bankruptcy to measure the bankrupt's income against his essential expenditure. The difference is known as the surplus income. A percentage of the surplus income is then paid into the bankruptcy estate (pot of money for creditors).

A similar approach can be used when managing your own finances. Following are two tables. One is a blank IPA table. Use this table to fill in all types of monthly income, and your **essential** expenditure.

Essential expenditure is the expenditure that **has** to be paid each month, such as rent or mortgage payments, petrol, food, etc. Don't put down non-essential expenditure (such as cigarettes). We will look at that next.

The first of these two tables gives an example of Bob's essential income against expenditure.

Bob's Income against expenditure		
Outgoings		
Mortgage/Rent		600
Housekeeping		250
Gas, Elec, Heating		150
Water		50
Telephone Charges		50
Travel to/from work		150
Clothing		50
Fines/Maintenance		0
Council Tax		112
Other Essential payments:		
Car Insurance	*40*	
Car Maintenance	*30*	
TV Licence	*11*	
-	-	
Other Essential payments		81
Total Outgoings	**(a)**	**1,493**
Income		
Monthly take home pay	**(b)**	1,833
Other household income	**(c)**	0
Total Income (b + c)	**(d)**	**1,833**
Surplus monthly income (d - a)		340

Your Income against expenditure

Outgoings
Mortgage/Rent
Housekeeping
Gas, Elec, Heating
Water
Telephone Charges
Travel to/from work
Clothing
Fines/Maintenance
Council Tax

Other Essential payments:

Other Essential payments
Total Outgoings   **(a)**

Income
Monthly take home pay   **(b)**
Other household income   **(c)**
Total Income (b + c)   **(d)**

Surplus monthly income   (d − a)

Following your chosen path of one of the remedies of debt explained in this book, you should no longer have any credit card or loan debts. With this in mind you should now have a surplus income. In other words your income should be greater than your outgoings. If it is not, it may be advisable to contact a citizen's advice bureau for further advice. It may be depending upon your personal circumstances that you are able to claim certain benefits.

Working on the assumption that you have a surplus income, and unless you are unemployed, you should. We will now look at your non-essential expenditure.

Following are two further tables. One is a blank table to list all the non-essential monthly expenditure that you currently spend. In the appropriate box insert the surplus monthly income calculated in the table above. Again, by way of example the first of these two tables has been completed by Bob.

Bob's non-essential expenditure		
Non-essential spend (NES)		
Cigarettes		40
Lottery tickets		10
Alcohol		30
Eating out		50
Entertainment		50
Satellite television		15
Holidays		30
Charities		5
Gifts		30
Hair/cosmetics		25
Subscriptions		10
Dental		10
Medical		10
Total NES	(a)	315
Income		
Surplus monthly income	(b)	340
New Surplus income (b – a)	(c)	25

Your non-essential expenditure		
Non-essential spend (NES)		
Total NES	**(a)**	
Income		
Surplus monthly income	**(b)**	
New Surplus income (b − a)	**(c)**	

As can be seen in the example above, due to Bob's lifestyle his surplus income has been cut down to just £25 per month.

Having listed all your non-essential expenditure you will probably be surprised to discover where all your surplus income is going.

Following are two further tables. In your table you need to eliminate expenditure that you feel you can do without each month and reduce expenditure where you feel that you can. It should not be necessary to eliminate all of your non-essential expenditure completely. After all, we need some luxuries in life. It is however important when reducing expenditure that although you want to keep expenditure to a minimum, you are realistic in your expectations of what you can achieve (willpower is essential). In the first of these two tables Bob has again listed his personal expenditure.

Bob's non-essential expenditure			
Non-essential spend (NES)			
Cigarettes		~~40~~	20
Lottery tickets		~~10~~	0
Alcohol		~~30~~	10
Eating out		~~50~~	25
Entertainment		~~50~~	20
Satellite television		15	15
Holidays		30	30
Charities		5	5
Gifts		~~30~~	15
Hair/cosmetics		~~25~~	15
Subscriptions		~~10~~	0
Dental		10	10
Medical		10	10
Total NES	(a)	~~315~~	175
Income			
Surplus monthly income	(b)		340
New Surplus income (b – a)	(c)		**165**

Your non-essential expenditure		
Non-essential spend (NES)		
Total NES	**(a)**	
Income		
Surplus monthly income	**(b)**	
New Surplus income (b − a)	**(c)**	

As can be seen in the example above, having made some small sacrifices and changes to his lifestyle, Bob can now put aside £165 per month in savings.

The above is a useful system in managing your finances and realising where your money is actually going each month.

If you wish to take this one step further, following is a useful system you may wish to adopt to ensure that you stick to your monthly spending targets outlined in the table you have just completed.

Next Step

Having produced your list of non-essential expenditure per month, write down the title of each expenditure type on the back of individual envelopes and the expenditure target that must not be exceeded.

Make sure you receive receipts for all purchases. If not then note down how much you spent on an item. When you get home, put the receipt in the relevant envelope and write down the amount you spent on that item on the back of the envelope. Keep a running total on the envelope so that you can make sure that you do not exceed your target spend. Managing each individual expense in this way will help you to keep within your targets.

As listed in the last table completed by Bob, he will have thirteen envelopes (although certain expenses such as holidays are just an allowance to save each month until he can afford his vacation). You may only have five or six envelopes. By way of example, following is how Bob's first envelope may look by the end of the month.

Cigarettes – Target £20

Date of purchase	Purchase price	Running Total
1 August	5.10	5.10
9 August	5.10	10.20
17 August	5.22	15.44
26 August	3.30	**18.74**

Bob had to purchase a pack of ten cigarettes in the last week of the month to ensure that he stayed within his target. However by managing each of his expenses in this way he was able to keep within all of his targets and managed to put the surplus income left over into his savings account.

Bob found that the small sacrifices he had made were very much worth the effort.

This method, although effective, is a tedious and time consuming task. However if you begin managing your finances in this way, even for just one or two months, it will set you into good habits and should make you far more aware of how easy it is to overspend and how, with a little bit of self discipline it is equally as easy to save money without making large sacrifices.

Following the steps above should ensure that you live a debt free life from now on.

The key to staying debt free is to ensure that you live within your means.

Finally

I am hoping my last advice will not be necessary. However if in the future you find yourself owing money to various credit card companies, following is an option you may wish to consider when working out the best route to repaying these debts.

Each credit card debt will incur interest month by month. If you have several credit cards you will likely not be in a position where you can pay off more than the required monthly minimum repayment each month. Therefore in order to repay these debts you need to approach them in the most cost saving way possible.

If you find yourself in such a position, list your credit card debts in the order of whichever card incurs the highest interest rate down to the lowest interest rate. Set up a table similar to the following table.

Credit card Co.	Interest rate	Outstanding balance	Minimum required	Payment	Balance

To prevent incurring further interest charges you must repay the minimum instalment on each card monthly.

In addition, in order to reduce your total credit card debts each month, you must pay at least one credit card over and above the minimum payment required. I suggest that you focus on the card that incurs the highest interest rate first and work your way down the list.

Epilogue

I hope you have found this book to be helpful and that I have helped dispel some of the lingering myths that only serve to perpetuate the unhelpful stigma attached to bankruptcy.

Some 100,000 people like Bob are likely to go bankrupt or enter some form of insolvency over the next year. If you extrapolate that over a decade it is likely that at least one of your friends or relatives will experience either financial problems or take part in one or more of the insolvency processes. Now that you have read BOB, I am confident that you will be well placed to help them take control of their finances or help dispel any fears they may have as to the insolvency processes or their consequences.

Appendix

Simple Individual Voluntary Arrangements (SIVA) [Abolished Scheme]

Shortly before the publication of this book the government abolished plans to introduce a proposed scheme for a simplified version of the IVA. This scheme was expected to be implemented in 2009. I have decided to include this chapter based on the proposals of the SIVA in the form of an appendix as this previously proposed scheme may be reviewed and perhaps implemented at a later date.

Similar to an IVA, a SIVA is a formal arrangement between an individual and his creditors. This applies to individuals with small debts and few assets, and the processes are accordingly simpler, and hence cheaper than the current option of an IVA. If it became available, the SIVA would be the preferable option for the smaller debtor.

Bob sought the advice of an Insolvency Practitioner (IP). Bob was informed that:

The current IVA scheme, as set out in part VIII of The Insolvency Act 1986, was originally intended for the likes of company directors, sole traders and members of professions. These cases tend to be quite complex and therefore accumulate large administrative costs to be paid to the IP appointed as Nominee and Supervisor of the IVA proposal.

Many more people have taken advantage of IVAs than those above, and for those individuals with small debts, the SIVA is likely to be the better option.

The problem with the IVA is that many people that enter into an agreement incur high costs for what should be a relatively straightforward case. This is because, as explained earlier, the intended target for IVAs was originally for the more complex cases.

There are procedures in place for IVAs which have to be carried out in all IVA cases. Due to this it had been decided that an alternative option should be available for people who have more straightforward financial circumstances. The proposed new procedure was the Simple Individual Voluntary Arrangement (SIVA). The SIVA was expected to be implemented and available as an alternative option to remedy debts as from April 2009.

In this example, Bob is employed as an Office Administrator and has debts of £52,000. Bob qualifies for the SIVA system (as will be explained below). Bob finds that the benefits of this system over IVAs are as follows:

- The new SIVA scheme is designed for people with debts of no more than £75,000. The idea is that this scheme will then accommodate the simpler cases that should not require the same level of administration as more complex cases involving significantly larger debts.

- In the Current IVA system, various papers have to be filed in court. This requires administrative time of the IP and therefore incurs extra expense. The SIVA scheme intends to eradicate the requirement to file papers in court and also to reduce other administrative procedures, thereby reducing the overall fees. The result of this is that all parties should benefit:

o   The IP, as the work involved should be reduced.

o   The court, as they will not have to receive and file such papers.

o   The creditors, as with reduced costs, they should receive a larger dividend from the contributions paid into the arrangement by Bob.

o   Bob, due to less formality and stress.

- In the current IVA system, a meeting of creditors must be arranged before the proposal can be approved. The SIVA scheme cuts out the requirement of a meeting of creditors. This again is a cost saving exercise. For the SIVA scheme IP's will send the proposal to creditors. Creditors can then either accept or reject the proposal. They cannot request changes as they would be able to do in a meeting for an IVA. This is a relief to Bob who did not want the added stress involved in attending a meeting and having to take on board requests from creditors to adjust areas of his proposal.

- In an IVA a vote of 75% in value of creditors must be received in favour of the IVA proposal in order for it to go ahead. For the SIVA proposal to be approved the IP must receive a majority vote from creditors, being 50% of the total value of creditors in favour of the proposal. This obviously benefits Bob as he does not need to reach agreement with as greater a percentage of creditors as he would in an IVA agreement.

- It has been proposed that there will be a 90 day time limit for creditors to lodge their claim. The purpose of this is to speed up the procedure and therefore reduce costs. It also means that creditors will receive their dividend earlier, as after the 90 days have elapsed there will be no need for the IP to hold back payments to creditors. Any creditors that file after this time will have missed the boat.

The proposal was approved following a majority vote from creditors in favour of the proposal. It was agreed that Bob would pay a fixed sum each month into the SIVA over a period of five years.

About the Author

Robin Meynell is a qualified Accounting Technician and has worked as an Examiner for the Official Receiver for the last four years. Robin has witnessed first-hand the difficulty experienced by people trying to obtain straight to the point information and guidance on the various remedies available to debt. Through BOB, he aims to share his knowledge and experience and to offer simple, practical guidance. He lives and works in Cambridgeshire and, perhaps ill-advisedly, supports Luton Town football club.

Printed in the United Kingdom by
Lightning Source UK Ltd., Milton Keynes
137195UK00001BB/25-42/P